Two Bucks and a Can of Gas

Model A Adventures
on the Gunflint Trail

Robert R. Olson

North Shore Press
Grand Marais, MN

Photos from Robert Olson's collection
Cover and text design by Breanna Super

U.S. Publisher
North Shore Press

Produced By
Northern Wilds Media, Inc.
PO Box 26   Grand Marais, MN 55604
(218) 387-9475
www.NorthernWilds.com

ISBN 0-9740207-5-3

Printed in the United States of America by Bang Printing

10 9 8 7 6 5 4 3

To my father, Richard Olson, and my grandfather, Alfred Olson, who helped me learn to take care of the Model A, but more importantly taught me to take care of myself in all seasons outdoors, and who recognized my desire to explore with what means we had. We never thought of ourselves as poor. Rather, we felt blessed to live a life in northern Minnesota.

Contents

Part 2: Gunflint Years

Acknowledgments

The literary and financial contributions of Dr. A. Paul and Carol Schaap made the publication of this book a reality. A special thank you to Calvin Stevens for providing storage for the Model A on the Gunflint Trail. Also a heartfelt appreciation to Keith Morris for inspiring and encouraging me to write these stories. Finally, and with utmost esteem and gratitude, I thank my wife, Kay, for interpreting my scribbling into a final document. Thank you. I've been both blessed and lucky to have true friendship. —*Robert Olson*

Introduction

When you are young, your ability to remember is immense. Also, you are impressionable. As decades pass, your ability to remember decreases and you are blessed with memories. At gatherings of families and friends, much time is spent recalling events, times and possessions. "Do you remember," "Whatever happened to," and "What did you do with" are three common phrases people repeat as they recall the past.

Besides memories, keepsakes are often either spoken for or handed down from one generation to the next. Keepsakes run the gamut from dishes, tablecloths, jewelry and furniture to war memorabilia, fishing tackle and guns. Some items have little monetary value; others are of significant value. Some items, regardless of value, are treasured and thought of as priceless. This latter attitude is often the result of memories.

So I write my memories about a 1930 Model A Ford truck. The Model A is a hand-me-down keepsake—not extremely valuable, yet priceless because it represents a lifetime of memories.

1

The Birth of the Model A

K A BOOOM! No sooner had I lit the match over the 50-gallon drum than I was engulfed in a colossal orange sphere of hot, burning gas.

The explosion occurred at an Olson family gathering in northern Minnesota. Payne, Minnesota, to be precise, located along the DM&IR tracks on Highway 7, halfway between Duluth and the Iron Range.

Excitement was in the air. I was 7. It was the fourth of July, 1952. Uncle Bill and family had come from California for a summer visit, bringing loads of fireworks from the western states. Firecrackers were the main staple, with rockets to be shot off after dark.

Soon after supper, the men—Uncle Bill, Uncle Kenny and Dad—started lighting firecrackers. Grandpa Alfred Olson sat on the railroad section house porch and watched. You know how it goes. First a single firecracker was lit, then two firecrackers twisted together, and so on. Pretty soon firecrackers were being placed under tin cans. When lit, this created a louder boom and more pandemonium accompanied with laughter. Soon it was my turn to light a single firecracker.

"His first firecracker! Get the camera!" someone yelled. Off it went without a hitch. Then another, and another.

Things settled down. All day I served as the gopher, or

errand boy, for the men who were reassembling a Model A pickup truck. Other relatives—from aunts and uncles to parents and grandparents—sat on the porch to visit and wait for nightfall and rocket time. The only thing that didn't settle down was me. My mind was hurtling with ideas on how to make a bigger boom.

While I thought, I helped with the Model A. The Model A, produced by Ford Motor Company from 1927-1931, was a vehicle with many interchangeable components, including motors, transmissions, rear ends, radiators, hoods, bumpers, springs and lights. What distinguished one vehicle from another was the body style. Options included a coupe, a four-door sedan, and a pickup.

By the end of the day, the men had assembled a running, reliable pickup. Before supper they enacted a successful 8-mile round-trip test run to Lake Nichols. A black Model A Ford truck was born.

Grandpa and I stayed behind to clean up the garage. You know—do this, do that, put this away, run these old rags to the big drum behind the ice house, that sort of thing.

I was still scheming about firecrackers. Not short on creativity, I concocted a scheme to produce a loud boom with an echo chamber—the 50-gallon drum behind the icehouse. (Who knows how the mind of a youngster works?) Off I went while joviality was happening on the porch. Across the top end of the drum, I placed a single firecracker with a clean, empty soup can, the open end over the explosive. That's how Uncle Bill had showed me on the sidewalk.

No one ever knew if the firecracker ignited. For when I

Grandpa's red Model A truck.

scratched the single matchstick on the emery board, the explosive fumes from the garage rags trapped in the drum shattered the peaceful evening with a salvo of furor and flame. The next day, the nearest neighbor—who lived five miles away—asked Grandfather what kind of fireworks had rendered the plume of black smoke and clap of thunder.

The experiment was a success, as far as I was concerned. However, the adults were unnerved. While fortunately my skin was not burned, every single hair on my body from the shoulders up was singed. Of most concern was my lack of eyelashes and eyebrows.

No one remembers if rockets were launched that evening.

I recovered. I never trusted a firecracker again. The black pickup, which became my pickup years later, was such a success that the men scrounged junk Model As to assemble one for Grandfather in his early retirement years. In order to tell the two pickups apart, they painted Grandpa's red.

2
First Ride

The following day, somewhat recovered from the previous evening's commotion, I accepted Dad's offer to ride 30 miles in the Model A to our home in Duluth. Younger sister Jan accompanied Mom in the family's 1948 Pontiac Silver Streak Coupe, providing escort service should trouble occur with the Model A.

Bob, Richard, Roberta, and Jan Olson with 1948 Pontiac Silver Streak.

Totally awestruck: That is how I felt during that ride. Sounds I'd never heard before: the roar of the engine at a top speed of 40 mph, the chatter of the transmission when pulling away from an intersection, the backfiring of the engine if the spark lever wasn't positioned properly, and the metal squeal of the mechanical brakes.

Dad was a master of the double clutch. First pushing the clutch pedal to the floor, pulling the shift lever to neutral, quickly letting the clutch out, and revving up the engine speed with the round quarter-size gas pedal on the floor. Now, while the engine was revved up, pushing in the clutch quickly and coaxing the shift lever to the next gear—either up or down—clutch out, accelerating to speed. All these actions were to mesh the engine speed with the transmission gearing speed. Messing up double-clutching produces a nasty clashing of gears (hopefully no transmission gear damage) and loss of momentum and who knows what else could happen going down steep hills in Duluth.

Shortly down the highway I began to detect an odd odor. Dad assured me that it was no problem. The smell was probably some excess grease melting on the engine. Soon the smell dissipated.

Next, even with both the crank-down door windows open, I shared with Dad that I was getting overly warm. With his left hand on the heavy black steering wheel, he guided the Model A down the road while at the same time reaching down in front of me by my feet. He closed the round door on the manifold heater. It was still extremely warm inside the truck. To my astonishment, he proceeded to push out the hinged windshield. I felt so proud of being able to lock and tighten the passenger adjustment lever on the windshield. Air conditioning, 1930-style.

At a certain speed, Dad noticed a slight wobble in the steering wheel. He chose a side road to pull off and asked me to get out. He removed the interior back cushion, got the wheel lug nut wrench out, and torqued the lug nuts on the front wheels. Sure enough, several nuts on the right front were slightly loose—an oversight on the July 4th assembly day. Lug nut wrench behind the back cushion, cushion secured, door closed, a complex miracle was observed: He restarted the engine.

Starting the engine required a series of actions demanding precise coordination. With the emergency brake engaged and the transmission in neutral:

Turn key on.

Push clutch pedal to the floor (it helps in cold weather).

Advance the spark lever on the left side of the steering post up.

Put the throttle lever halfway down on the right side of the steering post

Push the starter button on the floor to engage the starter, which starts the engine. Release quickly when the engine starts.

Quickly pull down the left-hand spark lever.

Adjust the throttle (engine speed) by pushing the lever up.

No choking for extra gas is necessary if the engine is warm. However, if both the engine and the weather are cold, turn the choke knob found in front of the passenger three turns to the left (counter-clockwise) and pull out while engaging the starter. When the engine is warm, close the choke.

Starting a Model A, especially in the winter, required deft timing and coordination.While a youngster, I watched my father and grandfather perform this process flawlessly summer and winter.

The Model A truck sat outside the single-stall garage at our family home on the hillside in Duluth. It performed faithfully in all seasons. Over the course of the next year, I discovered what its role was to be.

3
Autumnal Adventures

Hunt, fish, camp! Hunt, fish, camp! Our vehicle of choice was the 1930 Model A pickup, not the popular four-wheel drive vehicle or one of the gaudy station wagons that were emerging on the automotive horizon in the early to mid 1950s.

Who didn't hunt or fish during that time? Rural Minnesotans did, and did we ever hunt! It was a rare weekend from mid-September to Thanksgiving that we didn't spend time in the outdoors.

Most of the fall grouse hunting was done on the ditch-banks around Grandfather Olson's home in Payne. Ditchbanks were the results of the government's WPA (Works Progress Administration) effort during the Depression. In the lowlands of the area, the soil appeared an ebony color. Surely the soil would produce excellent crops, as ground moisture was abundant. On a platted one-mile grid, work "roads" were created by excavating soil, placing the soil on the "roadbed" and proceeding straight to the next one-mile quadrant. Since the water table was high in the area, water seeped into the ditch. Unperceivable, the water flowed, be it ever so slowly due to the flat topography of the area. Celery was introduced as a crop, but as a farming product it never sustained itself.

The WPA efforts years later may have been deemed unsuccessful as a farming practice, but they resulted in an intricate, flourishing wildlife mecca. It was on these ditchbanks I learned to drive the Model A, nurtured my fondness for the outdoors, and practiced gun marksmanship and safety under the tutelage of my father and grandfather.

Why did I always do well in school in the fall? Hunting on Saturday! The excitement to drive the ditchbanks! I never tested the parental warning "No hunting if the teacher calls!"

Glinting frost suspended from every piece of vegetation greeted us on many September Saturday mornings as we geared down to first gear in the A and turned onto our favorite ditchbank. After stopping to load his double-barrel 20-gauge shotgun, Dad would climb into the pickup box and Grandpa would drive.

Dad was ahead of his time. He designed and built a metal pipe rack that fit the stake pockets of the pickup box. While standing on the box floor and looking ahead on the trail, the rack kept him in place as the Model A inched forward along the trail. I sat in the cab next to Grandpa. The instructions to me were simple: "Roll down the window and watch for grouse under the balsams off to the side."

The blast of the 20-gauge would frequently startle me without any verbal warning. All it took to stop the forward progress of the Model A was for Grandpa to push in the clutch. Dad would jump out of the box and scurry, always searching with his eyes for another grouse, to snatch a flopping bird. It took me many years to spot grouse in the tall road grass. When the science teacher talked about animal camouflage I understood the concept perfectly.

When next fall grouse season arrived, I was bigger in stature and trained in gun safety. Gun safety was a discussion topic during haircuts. No sooner would I sit down in Dad's high metal workshop chair to have my hair cut (or my ears lowered) by Dad than he would hand me a card with the "Ten Commandments of gun safety". I would read; he would explain and state specific examples of each commandment. Over the summer I was given a well-cared-for bolt-action .410 shotgun. The following Christmas, to my complete surprise, Santa Claus delivered a new junior bolt-action .22 Mossberg rifle.

After much shotgun and rifle practice at Grandpa's the following summer, grouse season came and I was ready to ride the right front fender of the Model A. Fender riding! Fender riding with a real shotgun.

"Shoot him, Bobby," my grandpa would say as he halted the Model A's forward progress on the ditchbank. Not knowing where the bird was, nor wanting to disappoint either Dad or Grandpa because they were giving me a chance to shoot, I would quickly look at Grandpa's focused eyes and center my attention to the same area. By that time, the grouse would become skittish, strut or bob its head, revealing itself, giving me time to shoot. I don't know which one of us had a bigger smile after my first grouse—Dad, Grandpa or me.

Fender riding is exactly that—sitting on the fender while the Model A crawled along in first gear. The fender rider had several advantages over an on-foot hunter, including quick, easy access to stand on the ground for a shot, speedy transition to pursue a fleeing grouse into the woods, and, believe it or not, the ability to hear a grouse running on dry, fallen autumn leaves.

One could ride on the fender of a Model A for several reasons. First, the graceful curved shape of the fender was a very comfortable seated position located close to the ground. Second, the fully exposed headlight cross arm, running from the right front fender to the left front fender, provided a superb handle to hold if required. You only had to hang on with one hand, as the speed was turtle-like. You would rest the shotgun in your lap and hold it with your other hand. Finally, the bar bumper of the Model A furnished a strong, sturdy footrest. Even the occasional drift of heat from the exposed radiator felt comforting on chilly October days.

Today's vehicles provide none of the Model A's advantages. Furthermore, it is now illegal to transport a loaded, uncased gun in or on a vehicle.

Many years later, I remember the times when I yelled "Stop, grouse!" and jumped off. I was now a real hunter since I spotted, shot and retrieved a grouse without any adult assistance.

Sometime during the mid 1950s, scrap iron prices rose. Scrap-iron collecting joined grouse hunting as a weekend activity. Be it on a Saturday hunt or a warm, sunny Sunday after church, Dad and I would pack the shotguns in the Model A and head up Highway 7 to Grandpa's. Along the way, we would stop at long-abandoned homesteads and load the small Model A box with iron. Whether the site was an abandoned homestead, logging camp or dump, two iron items were common and heavy: cast-iron cook stoves and old abandoned vehicles. Often, while Dad broke down the scrap iron to a size that would fit into the Model A's box, I would walk with my .410 shotgun in the area. Often I came back with grouse and helped load the pickup with iron. Once we got home, we would unload the scrap iron in a big pile.

By the following summer, the scrap iron pile had mushroomed in size. Dad was getting heat from Mom that it had to go. At the break of dawn the next Saturday, Dad and I loaded the first of four loads that morning and headed for the scrap yard at the foot of the hill in Duluth's West End. We were the first to drive onto the scale that morning. Next we unloaded the iron by hand on the designated spot. (Dad was careful about sharp metal on the ground that could puncture a tire.) Then we drove back on the scale with a now scrap-iron-free truck. Dad parked on the street and went in and got his check. We promptly headed up one of the steep avenues that led to Piedmont Avenue. Once home, we took no break, just loaded and went. Luckily, we were able to get the four loads weighed before the noon closing on Saturday.

Once home I wasn't so lucky. Frequently I had observed Grandpa or Dad in the summer remove the radiator cap and add water to the radiator before starting the Model A. The task was routine, simpler than tightening the water pump packing nut and downright elementary compared to disassembling the water pump to replace the packing seal nut.

Why was the radiator gurgling like an old percolator? I wanted to find out. With both hands on the shiny chrome radiator cap, I gave a mere quarter-twist.

Searing steam gushed from the radiator cap opening like the Old Faithful geyser, instantly scalding my wrists and chest. Fifty-some years later, I still bear the scald marks. I ran screaming into the garage to Dad. Because it was a warm day and I had been working, all I was wearing on top was a t-shirt.

Without any hesitation, Dad pulled the scalding t-shirt off. Today the burn scars on my ribs have aged and vanished. The doctor said Dad was quick-thinking and saved me prolonged treatment for burns. That afternoon, although uncomfortable, I got to watch Dizzy Dean broadcast the baseball "Game of the Week" on black and white television.

Model A radiator caps didn't come with either pressure warning labels or push-down-and-twist safety caps as today's vehicles do. This was obviously another life lesson. I learned many lessons for life from childhood with the then 25-year-old Model A: learning by doing, not being afraid to try, not giving up, and being able to be myself and try things for myself.

Eventually another autumn approached. Shorter days, crisp nights, and brilliant autumnal pigments once again hastened my hunting desire. Circumstances this fall were both dismal and sensational. Grandma Olson was no longer alive. Cancer had taken her from us at 55 years of age. Even today I have visions of her taking an armload of kindling from me, putting most of it in the kitchen wood-fired stove box, adding a couple of kindling sticks to the stove, and flipping pancakes on top for me to eat.

Grandpa didn't join our Saturday hunts as often that fall. It was mostly Dad and me. Occasionally Jim Swanson, who worked with Dad, joined us. He was a soft-spoken, kind man from rural Wisconsin. With his help and salvaged timbers from Grandpa we built a few bridges across ditchbanks to gain access to the next quadrant for hunting purposes. These bridges consisted of a pair of 3-inch by 12-inch by 20-foot planks (one plank for the right-side tires, the other plank for the left-side

Crossing the ditchbank bridges.

tires) anchored to vertical cedar log pilings four feet above the waterline. I always lived in fear the Model A was going to slip off the planks and fall into the mucky, bog-stained water.

One adult standing on the opposite ditchbank would guide by pointing in the direction the wheels had to be turned to guide the Model A onto the wooden ribbons. Once one started across, a steady straight-ahead was taken until the rear wheels were on terra firma. Then we jumped on the fenders or in the box for another thrilling mile. Once I learned to drive the Model A I never, never, never attempted to cross one of those bridges. Even though once I got my driver's license I got stuck sometimes, I had enough sense not to venture over a ditchbank bridge.

That fall, I learned to drive the Model A on ditchbanks. Was I 10 years old? I really don't remember if I was that young. I do remember that Grandpa had sure made starting and shifting look easy. After a couple of attempts to get started and actually moving, I was no longer as confident with my "Yes" reply to Dad's question "Do you want to drive?"

From his standing position in the box, Dad gave the commands. "Spark up, no choke, throttle half down, clutch in, step on the starter, don't hold the starter down!" Success came in a roaring big way.

"Throttle up!" he yelled.

Anyone who has learned to drive a standard transmission has experienced the frustration I had for the next few moments to initiate forward motion. I can say this—at least no other drivers honked in frustration at my initial feeble driving attempts on the ditchbank.

Eventually the Model A jostled forward in motion. I had forgotten the entire purpose of this trip when a tumultuous double BANG BANG report from Dad's double-barrel 20-gauge shotgun startled me. Without thinking I took my foot off the floor accelerator. The Model A made a couple of jerks and stalled. Dad didn't really have to tell me I needed to push the clutch in. I learned by experience. He had shot two grouse, which I didn't even see. I was elated.

Eventually, commanding the black pickup down the ditchbank trails that fall was marvelous. I actually volunteered to chauffeur Dad, Grandpa, Jim, and even Mom and Jan when they joined us. The learning curve was steep and sensational. In the next few months, I eagerly accepted many responsibilities.

4

Mechanics 101

If you own or drive a vehicle, you must be able to mechanically take care of it. If you're hunting, fishing, or fetching a load of, say, firewood or scrap iron, you must be able to get yourself out of a jam. Help is not always available—and if is it, it is costly! So it was that my mechanical aptitude and fiercely independent way were born.

Hands-on learning doesn't just happen in the classroom. Learning Model A mechanics 101 helped me gain a lifetime of mechanical abilities. Among the rudimentary tasks I tackled were checking and changing oil, changing a flat tire, patching an inner tube, adhering a boot patch to a tire, adding distilled water to a 6-volt battery, changing a headlight bulb, tightening or replacing a fan belt, stopping a water pump leak, greasing a few pivot joints, adjusting the clutch, cleaning and changing spark plugs, cleaning a carburetor bowl, filling a differential or transmission, and adjusting the brakes.

A harder skill to learn was how to get myself out of a jam. At first I presumed it meant extracting a vehicle from a bog or maybe a snowy roadside ditch. If that were the case, a supplementary survival vehicle kit would include lengths of chain, an ax, a sturdy steel shovel, high lift jack, at least one mechanical jack (or better yet a hydraulic jack), a three-quarter-ton come-along, and blocking. But what if you were stranded by a severe engine failure? Or battery failure? Or...

Getting out of a jam often took ingenuity and creativity,

Bob inspecting the winch.

which experience taught. I learned many life lessons as an enthusiastic teenager with a Model A pickup. The Boy Scout motto "Be prepared" definitely applied. With events came experience, with experience came knowledge, and with knowledge came learning, Learning took time. Now I can say the best way to get out of a jam is to recognize the potential for dangerous situations and take precautions to avoid them.

5
Different Direction

Brimson, Fairbanks, Finland, Isabella. I had heard the names of these settlements, but that was all. Three years after the creation of the Model A pickup, in late August of 1955, Dad came home from a heavy-equipment repair trip excited about grouse hunting inland from Lake Superior, farther up the North Shore. He had spent the entire week rebuilding a road grader in the field, as service technicians say. Every day he saw numerous coveys of grouse. For that reason, we made plans to do our opening grouse hunting on the inland dirt trails.

This new direction set in motion my lifelong desire to explore. Many Saturdays found the two of us on the road out of Duluth headed for Two Harbors or old Highway 61. At Two Harbors we turned left—west, away from Lake Superior. With daylight approaching and several miles from Two Harbors, we made more turns. I had no idea where we were. Soon a road sign read "Brimson." But if this was a town, where were the houses, streetlights, stop signs and gas stations?

There were none. We were in the sticks.

Hunting was exceptionally good. This was a different style of hunting. We did much more walking on tote roads, as Dad called them. There were few other hunters.

That first day of hunting up the North Shore, I learned an important lesson in hunter ethics. Late morning, we came to what looked to be a prime tote road for grouse. It consisted of a couple of muddied truck ruts, patches of clover, intermittent tall grass, and a mix of balsam and poplar growth off to the sides.

One problem. A single vehicle sat at the road entrance.

Eager to ride down the trail as far as we could and then continue on foot, I pushed Dad to turn off and proceed. He would have nothing to do with it. He explained that maybe another father and son were hunting their favorite trail, just like we had our favorite ditchbanks. He went on to say ethical hunters respect other hunters and don't spoil the hunt by walking in behind them. He explained that if you wanted the privilege of hunting an area then you must get there first, even if that meant getting up an hour earlier. Besides, he went on to say as we heard a gunshot, they've scared off or shot the birds that were on the trail that morning. Oh, how I remember his comments. To this day I feel a high level of frustration when I'm backtracking from the end of a tote road and meet hunters who have entered the same tote road after me. Grr. Enough said.

Those Saturdays were extended days unless we got our limit of birds. We always brought sandwiches and goodies.

Bob practicing his shooting skills.

Coffee in a Thermos was a staple for Dad. I guess I had water. I never recall canned pop. Because we arrived back home in Duluth in the dark, tired, and also probably because of good hunting success, our once-frequent Sunday hunts were less so that fall.

Every Saturday hunting trip up the North Shore became longer in time and miles as we ventured on gravel roads as far as Finland—Finland, Minnesota, that is. Although back then I wasn't sure it wasn't the country of Finland, since a trip of that duration was 150 miles round trip at 30 miles per hour or less. It's funny, but I don't remember the trip logistics: gas supply, road names, truck maintenance, lunch, or even if I needed a hunting license.

One late October camping and hunting escapade etched distinct memories in my mind. Lured by the stories Dad repeated about Isabella Lake, Dumbbell Lake and Sawbill Landing, where he prepped Caterpillar heavy equipment for winter use that fall, we planned an extended weekend of exploring, hunting and camping. Only trouble was, we didn't own much camping equipment.

That didn't matter—we still went.

One thing I had was a sleeping bag. At the age of 11, I had joined the Boy Scouts. In the first two years, I participated in many overnight camping excursions. Because I enjoyed the adventures so much, I persuaded my parents to let me sell greeting cards door to door in the neighborhood. From a comic book advertisement, I had learned that if I sold 75 boxes of cards at $1.25 per box, I could earn a sleeping bag. Surprisingly, the all-occasion cards sold well once I explained my ambitious scheme. Soon my sleeping bag arrived. I was so proud. I used that sleeping bag for 20 years.

6
Cardboard Tent

Excitement rushed through my veins day and night the week before we left. Since it would be only a weekend trip, we had a fairly short list of items to pack before our early departure on a mid-October Saturday.

The plan was to hunt some of the best tote roads we had discovered on previous trips inland from Two Harbors, proceed north on gravel roads paralleling Lake Superior until we were in the Finland/Isabella area and then camp by Dumbbell Lake. On Sunday, we would reverse our path back to Duluth.

The heat from the truck's manifold heater lessened the pre-dawn chill on that October morning. Outfitted with a pair of dark brown cotton gloves, a light brown Jones hunting cap, and my first pair of 8″ leather boots (compliments of Dad), I felt comfortable in the frosty autumn forest.

Model A ready for fall hunting and camping trips.

Shortly after sunrise we spotted our first grouse. When the truck stopped I slipped out the door, slid a bullet into the open chamber, aimed, fired—and missed the standing grouse.

I had some explaining to do. Instead of using the .410 for the shot, I had chosen my .22 rifle. Why? The grouse looked so big, fluffed out and ready to strut, bigger than the tin soup cans I used for target practice. Why? At that time a single .22 rifle bullet cost only 1 cent compared to 10 cents for a single .410 shell. Why? Probably more excuses could have been used, but I still missed.

When I reentered the truck and slammed the door shut, Dad told me, "Use your shotgun. A hundred little pellets can be forgiving." I learned the value of a shotgun versus a rifle and a few other things in a brief, fleeting moment. I haven't missed much since, and when I do, my mind suffers a flashback in autumnal colors.

The day progressed nicely. A grouse here, a grouse there, very few hunters, great sandwiches, more clouds than sun, and thankfully no rain. All was well. Shortly after lunch, which we ate on a ridge overlooking Lake Superior, a brown wooden sign with yellow lettering on the shoulder of the gravel road pointed us in the direction of Dumbbell Lake.

The gravel roads had changed. They were no longer straight. Instead, they consisted of hills and sharp curves. Tall evergreen trees framed the road with an occasional creek just off the grassy shoulder. From vistas one could see the jagged topography of the North Shore. Amidst such magnificent sur-roundings, I actually forgot to concentrate on grouse until one ran across the leaf-littered road. That grouse filled my daily limit.

At the next junction in the road, another sign pointed us in the direction of the Dumbbell Lake Campground. Shortly we pulled into the deserted campground. Since we had never been to or through the campground we did the tourist thing. That is, we drove through the entire campground looking for the best campsite. It was my choice. I chose a picture-book site under magnificent pines close to the lake.

How simple it was back then. No reservation, no camp attendant, no fee, no billboard sign full of regulations. For many years to come, I was privileged to enjoy this unrestricted style of camping in northeastern Minnesota.

The water was a magnet. As soon as I had exited the cab of the Model A, I went to the water's edge. There was no dock, just undeveloped shoreline. Spiral-topped evergreens and partially golden leafed deciduous trees crowned resplendent hills. Croaking mergansers shuffled off and a distant plop on the water's surface hinted at finned life beneath. With so much to perceive, I hardly noticed the chill in the air.

Dad positioned the Model A for the night on the carpet of pine needles close to the picnic table. Before we set up camp, we took a hike with only my shotgun down the gravel road.

"Why only one shotgun, Dad?"

The gun was in case we saw a grouse. The primary purpose of the walk was to collect firewood away from the campground. We found dry wood not far away. After riding most of the day, the walk felt good. On our way back to the campground, an odd rabbit nibbled on plants along the shoulder. No grouse.

Back at the campsite, I was told to do a maintenance check

on the Model A. It was pretty simple—I lifted the left hood, showed Dad the oil dipstick (it was okay), and looked underneath for anything unusual. We would check the radiator in the morning when the coolant was at air temperature and no pressure existed. I learned that afternoon to never put off a maintenance check.

With instructions and a bow saw I quickly made a pile of firewood. I was told it was enough for a crackling campfire that night, but not enough for a toasty hand-warming morning fire.

This time I was sent down the road by myself. When I returned, I cut the wood to length and got instructions to put the wood under the picnic table with a piece of old canvas over it. We always carried odd pieces of canvas in those days; plastic tarps were not invented yet.

"Why cover the firewood, Dad?"

Time for another lesson. We covered the firewood to keep moisture, dew/frost, or even rain from getting to the wood, which would make it hard to start a fire in the morning. If the picnic table hadn't been there, we could have put the wood under the cab of the Model A.

A feeling of trust welled within me when Dad suggested I take the 22 rifle and see if the rabbit was still along the road. "Aim for the head" was his instruction. I'm sure I never heard "Take your time, aim carefully, don't go into the woods, and be careful!"

I had never shot a rabbit before. Two or three hundred feet down the road I was astonished. I wasn't even close to the rabbit spot yet, but here was a plump, strutting grouse in the ditch. Should I go back for the .410? No! I must remember from this morning's misfire to aim with exceptional focus.

Bang. I did it! It wasn't a head shot and there wasn't much flapping either. More questions. What about the rabbit?

I covered the grouse with my brown Jones hat and without hesitation went looking for the rabbit. Sure enough, I spotted the now partially white snowshoe hare close to the same location. Sneaking slowly, setting every foot down with care, I moved forward until the rabbit snapped to full attention. I was focused and the shot was accurate. I was jubilant, and I was transformed into a hunter, just as human beings—many with far cruder instruments than mine—have passed the survival test throughout history.

Carefree, I hustled rabbit and grouse back to the campsite. In the past 10,000 years since the last glacial period in northeastern Minnesota, could a young boy have run back to a camp in this area with his bounty? Absolutely. Perhaps he was met with the same elation by his elders as I was.

A considerable amount of learning was about to happen. Dad explained that the grouse would be part of my possession limit for the weekend. My daily limit had been filled, but Minnesota statutes at that time allowed for a possession limit. Tomorrow we would be allowed one less bird.

My happiness was somewhat tempered. Nevertheless, Dad's emotions were festive.

Cleaning a grouse was nothing novel for me. We always saved the breast, back, and legs. Before the snowshoe hare was cleaned, I learned about protective coloration and seasonal coloration transformations, a must for survival. Intently I studied the clean cuts with a jackknife and pulled the hide off the rabbit's carcass without a single drop of blood or guts. Next came a couple more cuts to separate the entrails from the body.

The raw skin of the rabbit I cherished and kept for some time after the camping trip. For a while, the rabbit skin remained flexible. Finally it hardened. There was something unique about the fur. In those days, fur and animal pelts were valued. I was proud of it until I took it to school to show friends.

That was a mistake. The girls shrieked and thought it was repulsive. A couple of boys made fun of it and me.

Many years later, my initial sense of the rabbit skin's value was validated when I made friends with Irv Benson, who lived on Saganaga Lake on the Canadian border. I had learned about Irv and his wife, Tempest, from Gunflint Trail residents. I had read about him in the 1960s in an issue of National Geographic and even seen a television documentary program about him.

As he and I sat in his Saganaga Lake home on a bitter January day, he shared many stories with me. He gave much credit to his wife, Tempest, for learning the ways to live on Saganaga Lake. He shared the story of a life-threatening trapping trip when a blizzard stranded them between trapping shacks on their trap line. They had to seek shelter; their footwear was saturated from slushy conditions on lakes and rivers. Tempest set out rabbit snares, caught rabbits, skinned them, and made fur-lined socks from the fur by turning the rabbit skins inside out. Irv told me he would not be walking today if not for Tempest and her skills with rabbit skins.

But back to the story. Engrossed so much in the skinning

of the rabbit and dispensing with the entrails down the gravel road in the opposite direction, it wasn't until I returned to camp that I realized Dad had cleverly prepared our sleeping quarters... in the tiny box of the Model A pickup! Quite a feat, for the box measured 41.5 inches wide and 48 inches long.

When we left Duluth early that morning, I hadn't known what lay under the heavy gray canvas that covered the box. The canvas was now draped over the pipe racks. The pipe racks, mounted in the stake pockets of the pickup box, were cab height in the front stake pockets and a foot high in the rear stake pockets.

The canvas stretched from the cab visor to approximately two feet past the end of the box. It extended down the sides to the top of the rear fenders. It was held in place by opening both cab doors, placing the canvas in the door opening, and closing the doors on the canvas. Before retiring that night, we put shotguns, food, and other non-clothing items in the cab. We tied the canvas at the rear to the pipe rack in case a wind arose.

How do you support a 6-foot person on a 48-inch length of floor? For this, a nearly 41-inch wide by 48-inch long extra piece of plywood (which Dad had cut to fit the pickup box floor) was extended rearward over the box's tailgate. In those days, tailgates were held in place by two chains, one on each side.

However, what stood out most of all was the cardboard. At his work in the shipping department, Dad had access to huge sheets of cardboard. During the past week, after our family supper, while I did homework, he folded, scored and cut a cardboard lining for our cocoon. One piece of prefab cardboard covered the floor, the tapered sides, and back of the cabin. He had cut to width and length one extra sheet that supported the overhead canvas and kept it from drooping or sagging on us.

I was alright with our shelter to that point. My new sleeping bag was rolled out alongside a Korean-War-vintage, U.S. Army-issued sleeping bag borrowed from my uncle Kenny. Perplexed, I did have to ask what the two heavy wool mats were laid out along the sides. Horse blankets, Dad said. Young, naïve, and not daring, I asked no further questions.

The day was a success. Our camp was in order. With the remaining daylight, it was time to focus on supper. Being a tenderfoot, this was not my responsibility.

On previous late-fall hunting trips, I had tasted hot pork and beans at lunchtime. These pork and beans acquired their heat while strapped to the manifold against the engine under the Model A's hood. This device, which held a couple of tin cans, was just one of many aftermarket accessories designed for the versatile Model A. Sadly, it did not come with a can opener and spoon.

That October evening our main dish, beef stew, was prepared on a Coleman cook stove. The name "Coleman" is virtually synonymous with camp stoves. These durable, time-tested stoves are known to perform on white gas year-round. Who has not seen a green two-burner Coleman with red legs?

However, it was not the customary green two-burner Coleman that we used, but instead a unique single-burner unit. It was unique because the cylindrical stove was stored in an aluminum dual-purpose canister. The canister consisted of a larger lower section and a smaller interlocking twist top. The top served as a traveling case to protect the stove and provide two different sizes of practical cooking pots. In each section was a recessed slot to insert a removable handle. The handle was stored along with the stove inside the canister for transportation.

The compact single burner stove operated on the same principle—white gas under pressure—as other Coleman models. Exceptional chrome metal stove materials guaranteed lasting quality. Fifty years later, I still use the same stove.

So well designed was this stove that a funnel came attached via a light chain so you could not lose the funnel. The funnel was for filling the spacious fuel reservoir. Operating instructions are stamped in the metal rather than on some decal that gets abused and becomes illegible.

Only once have I seen another model like it. I purchased it at a rummage sale without asking the owners any questions. At home I fueled it up and it performed flawlessly. It has no model number, but on the outside of the large pot/canister it says "Coleman Made in the U.S.A." It may not be as light as modern one-burner units, but I'm not trading.

After all the hot beef stew we could eat, we prepared an evening campfire. We kept the fire small intentionally since I was to learn how to roast a wild rabbit. With the initial fire burned down to coals, the rabbit was skewered on a green stick and propped above the embers. Between discussion topics, the rabbit was turned and a small stick or two of firewood was added to maintain consistent heat. It was astonishing how much light the coals and diminutive flame of the fire gave off once our eyes adjusted to the darkness. The rabbit was chewy but tasty. The discussion topics varied. Of utmost interest to me was chit-chat related to the coming deer season, something that I had been too young to participate in prior to this year.

Other than our voices, the only sounds to be heard were the crackles and pops of the campfire. No distant, mournful wails from a loon, no whispering pines, not even a rustle of leaves from an occasional scurrying mouse. Silence...until a piercing clamor came high from a dead popple snag at the entrance to the campground.

The strangled sounds paused briefly before starting up again from another tree less than 50 feet away. Now the sounds became intense, with plenty of gurgling and gargling. The collection of robust reverberations lasted for minutes. Then stifling stillness returned.

Chilled with fear, surprise and the frosty temperature, I whispered to Dad, "What was it?"

"An owl," he replied confidently. "Probably a great horned owl."

It was certainly no "Who cooks for you allllll" barred owl, I thought to myself. With my heart pounding and permission given, I threw three or four more pieces of firewood on the glimmering embers. As the restored flames grew high and more intense, so did my confidence.

Have you ever noticed on a cold evening how a campfire overly heats one side of the body while the other side of the body suffers the reverse sensation? After more discussion, listening for nature sounds, and turning away from the fire to heat my backside, it became obvious it was time to retire. The water in the washbasin from the lake sure felt cold on my face and hands. After I brushed my teeth and rinsed my mouth with icy water, my teeth began to chatter. Back to the campfire to warm face and hands over the crimson coals. Nudging un-burned log and stick ends into the center of the fire produced the last small fingers of flames. While turning and warming my hands and face, firelight reflected off the bumper of the Model A some 30 feet away.

Sitting there facing the fire, the Model A had a human-like, cartoonish, happy appearance. Firelight reflected off its features: The stubby windshield visor formed eyebrows, the two headlights with glass lenses portrayed real eyes with keen sensitive vision, sitting between the eyes and somewhat lower was the stout radiator or formidable nose, still lower the wide bumper pretended to be the cheerful mouth.

As for our sleeping quarters, well, two adults could not have laid side by side in a 41.5-inch opening. However, one adult and an 11-year-old boy could. Earlier, before the sun had set, Dad and I did a test fit. We knew it was possible. Now the trick was to get into the sleeping bags, partially clothed, in confined quarters, with a single flashlight as a source of light.

I was first to try. Right away I discovered a flaw in my sleeping bag in such cramped quarters. The zipper was only 30 inches long, which was no problem for an agile 11-year-old in a large Boy Scout tent. But in a cramped cardboard cocoon, it was slightly more difficult to enter while wearing wool socks, long underwear, sweatshirt, and a stocking cap perched on my head. I gave Dad as much room as possible lying on my side compressed against the side of the Model A's box.

Because his sleeping bag had a full-length zipper, he got in much easier than I had. He spread the horse blankets over the top of both sleeping bags. For a pillow, I balled up a jacket. The cardboard under us provided a fairly soft lining, did add insulation, and proved slippery enough to scoot a bit. The two-cell flashlight supplied ample light on the cardboard interior. Before it was turned off for the night, I observed that our feet extended beyond the hanging canvas overhead. Still, the horse blankets covered our feet and bodies up to our shoulders. With all the extra squirming getting in, I was completely warmed. Sleep came easy. It was some day.

The night passed quickly. The following morning, only my face stuck out of the sleeping bag. One eye told me it was daylight. The tip of my nose when I inhaled told me it was cold. The frozen breath from my mouth told me it was winter. I must have wriggled, because soon Dad pronounced the lumberjack ritual, "Daylight in the swamp!"

Both of us lay motionless for moments in our makeshift housing in the box of the Model A. I was the first to wriggle my head enough and shout, "Dad, there's snow on us!" In our sound sleep overnight, neither of us had realized it was snowing. Covering the foot of our sleeping bags was 3 inches of the white stuff.

We had been prepared. The horse blankets kept us warm, the cardboard likewise, plus it held the overhead canvas in place. The campfire wood was collected and dry, and all other supplies and necessities were stored in the cab of the truck. How different the Model A appeared in a blanket of white next to Dumbbell Lake that October morning.

Fringe ice clung to the shore, warning of the arrival of the next season. It was challenging to obtain camp water that morning. Slippery conditions prevailed on shore and underfoot around camp. Soon the Coleman stove provided tempered water for our needs.

A ritual transpired that morning: coffee. Never had I been offered a sip of coffee. Now it was a warm substitute for my cold Tang orange juice. Soon a cup of dehydrated milk was prepared to put over a generous helping of cooked oatmeal and raisins. Breakfast complete, we turned our attention to breaking camp and hunting our way back to Duluth.

Before the final walk-around camp inspection, we directed our attention to the Model A. Last night we had performed a routine service check. All that was required before starting this morning was to check the radiator. Dad removed the chrome radiator cap and peered at the top of the radiator core. Next, it was my turn to confirm a slightly low level.

Being fall, water couldn't be added to the radiator as the water would freeze solid, expand, and cause a serious radiator leak. Behind the seat cushion in the cab was a container of pure Prestone antifreeze. We mixed a 50/50 antifreeze-to-water solution in a quart container and filled the radiator so the core was covered. Too much solution and it would expand from the engine's heat and overflow onto the ground. We both got in the cab. I observed the cold starting technique of turning the choke knob three revolutions to the left and pulling out the choke rod while performing the starting miracle. Three, four, five, six growling engine revolutions occurred before the engine coughed and proclaimed a victory over the cold night.

The return trip to Duluth that Sunday was lackluster. We saw absolutely no grouse. With 3 inches of snow on the road and in the ditches, all the customary edible grouse vegetation was buried. Nor could grouse pick gravel for their gizzards. Had it not been for a variety of animal tracks that crossed or meandered down the back road, I could have easily fallen asleep sitting in the stream of the engine heat coming from the manifold heater. At least a half dozen times we paused, got out of the Model A, and observed deer, moose and impressively large wolf tracks. Several times rounding curves in the road we expected to see wildlife, but none materialized. As we got closer to Two Harbors, Highway 61, and Lake Superior the layer of snow on the ground diminished to nothing.

Without a doubt, the weekend was my most influential childhood outing. The experiences, observations, and knowledge I had garnered sowed the seeds of ambition to explore further and further. The desire to camp was nurtured. A sense of freedom was inspired and born. The Model A Ford played an integral part in the outing and was the hub of trips for years to come.

7
Winter Preparations

The overnight hunting and camping trip basically closed the season on grouse hunting. We spent a weekend at home in Duluth preparing for winter. Push lawn mowers, window screens, garden hoses and tools, and summer clothes all had to be put away in storage. Out of storage came metal snow shovels, snow scoops, storm windows, bird feeders, winter jackets, caps and boots, and furnace filters.

Even the Model A required a change-over and check-ups. A highly important task that promoted easier winter starting was changing the oil. In the fall a lighter viscosity weight, #10 oil, replaced the thicker viscosity summer-weight, #30 oil. In those days there was no multi-weight oil, such as 5W30. I remember Dad taking a 5-gallon can to an oil distributor and having it filled with re-refined oil of appropriate viscosity for the upcoming season. A quart of re-refined oil cost 15 cents. For less than one dollar you could change your own oil. Were we far ahead of the recycling trend? We returned our used oil and purchased fresh, clear oil in a container that was used repeatedly. No fuss with plastic quart bottles.

Many vehicle owners years ago had two sets of tires for the rear wheels. The two sets consisted of quiet running tires and noisy, aggressive snow tires. Since most vehicles were rear wheel drive, the appropriate tire sets were installed for the season. With the advent of better snowplowing, application of sand and salt to the roadways, and most of all the advance-

The Model A had a no-frills dashboard.

ment in tire technology to all-season tires, the practice of seasonal tire changing has mostly become a thing of the past.

We never had an extra set of tires for the Model A because we used it off the paved roads so much that we left on our traction tires, called "knobbies," all year. Knobbies provided more grip on dirt and in muddy conditions.

Another vital winter preparation was testing the antifreeze. (Did you ever use a simple testing device consisting of a round ball suspended in a solution for testing your radiator?) Nothing would render a Model A (or any vehicle) more worthless than a cracked block. A block refers to the main mass of the engine. Antifreeze coolant circulates in the engine block to reduce engine heat. The cooling system, at the heart of which is the radiator, was not always leak-proof when it aged. Thus it would require more fluid. In the summer, when the chance of overheating and loss of coolant was high, owners would often add water to the radiator. This practice would weaken the antifreeze solution and present a high probability of a cracked engine block over the course of a winter in the northern half of the United States. Thus, every fall, the strength of the antifreeze had to be tested. Dad believed the antifreeze had to be good to 40 below.

Which is damn cold! 35-40 degrees below zero on a thermometer! It is not just radiators and engine blocks that will crack at those temperatures. Batteries will also crack.

Standard on a Model A was a non-sealed 6-volt battery. In the early 1930s, batteries were not sealed; they required maintenance. Periodically the owner would have to check the battery cells to see that the acid level was above the lead plates. This maintenance check seemed to be required more in the heat of summer, or when the voltage regulator was out of adjustment.

If the acid level was low, a carefully measured amount of distilled water would be added. Alternatively, rainwater could be added. It was believed that rain water, much like distilled water, was free of the minerals in tap or ground water that would eventually shorten the life of a battery. Too much water would weaken the sulfuric battery acid and produce a dead battery with the potential of freezing and cracking the battery case.

Model A batteries were located under the floorboards on the driver's side. For ease of battery maintenance, protection from road debris such as sticks, flying rocks and ice, and a warmer surrounding environment in the winter, Dad made a bracket to hold the battery and mounted it to the firewall under the hood.

8

November Ritual

Did you have a childhood fear? I did. It was not terror; it was more of a scared feeling. Its triggers were nighttime, darkness, unlit garages, creaky doors, flashlights and hanging dead deer.

Deer hunting was an Olson family tradition. The clan hunted the edges of the swamps on the ditchbanks north of Duluth. At the end of each day, the shot deer were dragged to the Model A and either strapped over the front fenders or loaded into the box and hauled a couple of miles to Grandpa Olson's garage. Before supper the men would hang the deer from the rafters in the garage. The deer were safe in the garage from wild predators.

Inevitably, after supper, something—a red lunch bag, a hunting coat, a pair of wet mitts, a Thermos - would be forgotten in the garage. I would be handed a flashlight to retrieve it and reminded to make sure the door got latched. Of course, my very young age had to do with my apprehension. Then there was the fact that the garage was a fair distance away from the house, as was the custom in rural America years ago. Yard lights didn't exist, it was dark outside, the men spoke of seeing wolf prints, and the garage had no electricity. These were all fear factors.

Mustering up courage to enter the dark garage was a challenge. The small yellow beam of the flashlight caught the ghostly shape of hanging deer. As the flashlight beam scanned

Richard, Ken, Alfred and Bob Olson with one of the ditchbank bucks.

the bodies, ghastly shadows of the animals loomed even larger on the wall behind them. Casting the beam of light on the animal heads raised goosebumps over my body when the eyes reflected an eerie green. The odor of fresh blood pools beneath the deer and the pungent, musky tarsal gland permeated the one-stall garage. Somehow, I gathered enough strength to locate the wanted item. With no hesitation, item in hand, I scrambled to exit quickly.

As I got older, the scared feeling subsided. Was it because I got older or because I participated in the deer hunts? Probably both.

Feeling no apprehension, only excitement, family members and I prepared for my first deer hunt in the weeks following the Dumbbell Lake hunting and camping trip. A ritual a couple of weekends before deer season opened was to check our traditional hunting stands. Located on the edge of a huge cedar swamp near Payne, the stands were a challenge to access. After lunch was made, we loaded a generous supply of shorter lengths of used lumber, a hammer, long spikes, a hand saw and hatchets into the Model A pickup box. The hunters were bound for the woods.

On this trip and during deer season, Dad always drove the Model A, probably because of the nasty navigation that was required to travel around obstacles on the slippery, snowy ditchbank. The only time of the year we traveled on this ditchbank was to gain access to the deer stands.

The first trip was the worst. We encountered radiator-cap-high thistles, purple asters, and thorny raspberry stalks. Both willow and alder shoots were mowed down by the front bumper. Each year the trail narrowed due to overhanging popple and balsam branches. We always had to stop and chop or remove a few trees that had fallen across the trail.

Eventually, after a mile, we came to the only spot wide enough to turn around the short Model A. With no power steering ("arm strong steering," as it was called) and bog on both sides, Dad maneuvered the Model A. Frequently tire chains were used for extra traction.

The men—Grandpa, Uncle Kenny, Jim Swanson, and Dad – had all had their favorite locations and stands for years. Each stand had to be checked for safety purposes. Some required a few new boards or better steps. Occasionally, a new stand had to be built because a tree fell on the old stand. All shooting lanes had to be pruned. Some stands had names: Leaning Cedar, Three Cedars, Creek Stand. The stands were a quarter to three-quarters of a mile in various directions from the parked Model A.

Based on the deer sign, a site for any stand was chosen. Grandpa made a lot of deer stand decisions: location, direction to face, height, how much to clear, and how to get to the deer stand. I was a sponge for information, listening and learning from a patient master. When the stand was complete, we returned to the Model A for lunch. We would not return until the opening day of deer season.

Never did we have to worry about other invasive hunters. That's the way it was back then. The other area gangs, as Grandpa called them, had their traditional hunting areas. They would only venture into our area if tracking a wounded animal. Old-time hunter ethics.

Serious stuff! The Friday night before the opening of deer season, it was common for all hunters and any interested family members to stay overnight at Grandpa's. Final plans for Saturday were made, clothes laid out, lunches made, alarm clock set, and even the coffee pot readied. The goal was to be on our stands a half-hour before daylight.

At the sound of the alarm the hunters dashed through their paces like firemen. I'll always remember the faces: the warmth and friendliness of Uncle Kenny, the helpfulness of Jim, the serious looks of Dad. Even after breakfast, the regimen continued with few words.

One could sense the excitement of all when someone yelled, "Fresh 3 inches of snow overnight!" The plan was for Dad and me to ride together in the Model A and the men to follow in a second vehicle until we got to the ditchbank. At that point, Grandpa rode on the fender and the other hunters stood in the box for the ride to the parking area.

Grandpa and Jim with their flashlights headed for their deer stands in one direction. I followed Dad and Uncle Kenny across a frozen bog to my stand. They both helped me at my stand. I was given short, straightforward directions before they departed. Since Uncle Kenny's stand was closest, he assured me he would check on me by eleven o'clock.

Daybreak was beautiful. While I sat in the predawn darkness, I actually closed my eyes. To prevent the chills, I nestled my head deep into my collar, folded one arm over the other, and tucked my knees together. Occasionally, when I detected a noise, I would peer out. Soft and subtle the light of dawn spread throughout the forest, revealing identifiable objects in black and white. Soon, with the advancement of the sun, birds of winter flittered about in search of sustenance. Finally, brimming with sunlight, a winter spectrum of hues materialized.

With the arrival of daylight came many sounds. Some were easily identified; others were not. Some were distant; others were close. Some were soft; others were loud. Some provoked thought while others raised alarm. Here is a random inventory of sounds I perceived while perched on the deer stand:

A very distant volley of gunshots

A downy woodpecker tapping a dead birch

Falling snow pellets landing on cedar fronds

A jet passing high above, trailed by its engine roar

A scolding squirrel

A rumbling pickup muffler in the distance

A twittering flock of redpolls alighting in a high popple

The wind stirring the tops of trees

The flutter of a chickadee landing on the closest limb

The sharp snap of a dead branch breaking

A single, explosive, startling gunshot extremely close

A raucous wing-flapping raven

My own rapid pounding heartbeat

Approaching crunching footsteps

Variety of vocals from Canadian jays or gray jays

Muffled sandwich-wrap sounds

With so many stimulating sounds to assess on opening day, the loss of sleep due to an early awakening was not a problem. However, the onset of chills was a concern because it prompted squirming, fidgety motion.

Many times prior to today, I had been warned to stay concealed, as a passing deer could detect movement, and movement could create unnatural noise that would alert the deer to one's presence. How true, because I heard Kenny's crunching footsteps approaching before he emerged from the line of evergreen trees.

He whispered in soft, hushed tones, asked relevant questions, and stated that the extremely loud, close gunshot to the west had been Dad's. He presumed he shot a deer. He was also confident Grandpa had success. He helped me get down with utmost gun safety in mind. Noticing I was shivering, he suggested we hike to the Model A.

As we approached the Model A, we both noticed Grandpa and Jim struggling to lift a magnificent buck into the box of the pickup. I'm not sure I made much difference in lifting the buck, but Kenny did. Since it was early afternoon, Grandpa suggested we return to our stands. He planned to skirt the swamp, possibly chasing a deer in our direction. It was agreed to meet at the truck at 4 p.m.

The afternoon passed quickly and uneventfully. No longer chilled, and quite full from lunch in the afternoon sunlight, my head nodded until I could no longer hold my eyes open. Sleep overcame my desire to watch guard. Shortly before 4 p.m., Dad came down the trail to get me. He shared his success and we ambled to the truck. On the way to the truck I checked the deer trail I oversaw the entire day. No tracks! Good. Nothing snuck past while I snoozed.

Dad's deer was loaded on and strapped to the right front fender. What a memorable sight as Dad jockeyed the truck in the narrow turnaround. The other men had already started to walk out because the box had no real standing space left. Once back at Grandpa's garage, the deer were hung from a rafter. Working in pairs, the skilled hunters quickly skinned the hides from the animals. Supper was ready.

Hardly any of the hunters could stay awake after supper. Up early, outdoors in frigid temperatures, and dragging deer drained the energy of the hunters. Even though all were in bed before nine o'clock, it still felt like a very short night the following morning when the alarm clock rang.

The Sunday morning routine was an identical repeat from Saturday until we prepared to traverse the ditchbank. Instead of riding in the Model A's box this moonlit morning, Grandpa was going to wait half an hour until daylight and hunt his way into the deer stand area. He hoped to spook some deer into moving past the deer stands. What this did was allow me to ride in the box with Kenny.

In the small cab of the truck, Dad and Jim sat shoulder to

shoulder, garbed in overstuffed vests and red wool coats. In the headlight beam, glittering frost floated from the tall, tawny grass and branches. To the west, the full hunter's moon peered through gaps in the cedar branches. To the east, a faintly glowing horizon foretold a spectacular sunrise.

Next, I don't know which was more impressive—the sight of a buck leaping across the ditchbank in the headlights or the sight of a feathery red-orange 2-foot-long muzzle blast emitted from the barrel of Kenny's rifle.

Previously I had seen deer run across the highway in front of a vehicle at night, but this seemed so much closer in the frosty atmosphere of the narrow trail perched in the box of the truck. Etched forever in my vivid memory is the intense brilliance of the muzzle blast, just like images on a camera's film. Wow! Movie stuff!

Mid-morning, Kenny and Jim recovered the buck. Both Dad and I sat in our stands until near noon when Grandpa arrived from his push through the cedar swamp. No more deer sightings. Early afternoon, Kenny's deer was loaded into the box of the Model A and we headed for the garage.

Deeper arctic air and measurable snow brought an end to the successful deer season. It would be at least three years until I filled my license. Every season brought new experiences, skills and knowledge.

9

Boyhood Dilemma

Subsequent weekends through February took on a particular endeavor: ice fishing. Once again the black Model A pickup was summoned to duty.

The truck took the drudgery out of multiple tasks. Regardless of the wintery wind and weather conditions, the truck always started. It towed the wooden fish house out on the lake and off the lake in drifted, crusted snow. With its high clearance and narrow front wheels, it broke open a trail to the fish house where other vehicles failed. Should the snow become exceptionally deep, slushy and drifted, a set of tire chains secured to the rear wheels provided unbelievable traction. So good was it in snow, a snow shovel—which was always carried—was seldom used.

For the next three or so years, before I was eligible to apply for a Minnesota driver's license, I accompanied Dad and sometimes the aforementioned men on various forays in which the Model A was our means of transportation. Exploration for hidden lakes, brook trout streams, and remote grouse habitat beckoned us. During these forays, both summer and winter, we would encounter impassable trails. Too often, we spent hours extracting the Model A from what seemed like bottomless swamps or bumper-deep snowdrifts. It was during these journeys I learned the value of various simple hand tools and mechanical devices. These years provided valuable training and confidence for the abundant dilemmas of the years to come.

One such dilemma resulted from not being able to be outdoors on a mid-February Saturday. Being cooped up drove me to make a stupid decision on Sunday. Since my parents were gone for the entire day, I presumed I could take the Model A, travel 30 miles one way to Lake Nichols to ice fish and be home before the parents got back. I was 14 at the time.

It was a poor decision for many reasons: I had no Minnesota driver's license, I let no one know of my plans, I brought no lunch provisions or extra winter garments, and, worst of all, I brought along an 11-year-old neighborhood friend.

Before 10 a.m. on Sunday morning, I had called my friend. He was very willing to go and wasn't questioned by his parents. Being an average and sunny mid-February day, the temperatures were moderate. The road conditions were good. Soon we were on our way north out of Duluth.

I didn't think it right to travel the main highway—53— north to Lake Nichols so I opted for a lesser-traveled rural blacktop road. The drive was going smoothly: enough gas, little traffic, and, of course, the little black truck negotiated every curve in the road. I practiced and obeyed the rules of the road, even rolling down the window and arm-signaling turns (Model A trucks had no turn signals). Soon, however, I made an extremely poor decision—not that I had made any good decisions that day. I decided to take a 2-mile side road. This side road accessed two farms before it came out on the blacktop road again. It was going to be a short side excursion.

Several times in the past we had traveled this gravel road while grouse hunting. It ran one mile west before making a

90-degree right turn. From that point it ran one mile north to the blacktop road junction. Both at the beginning and end of the gravel road were two farmhouses. The occupants of the farms used the road to access their fields adjacent to the road.

Shortly past the first farmhouse that mid-February day, the road ceased to be plowed. The amount of snow on the road didn't appear any deeper than the snow on a frozen, wind-swept Minnesota lake. Without any hesitation I proceeded and did fine in second gear.

Soon the higher, windswept flat land gave way to much lower land. With no sense of alarm, the Model A descended a modest hill until it reached a hollow. Forward progress and momentum halted shortly thereafter. Shifting to reverse gear failed to budge the vehicle. We were stuck three-fourths of a mile from our entry point in winter snow accumulation. In the hollow the snow was bumper-deep. No longer did the wind sweep the snow off the roadbed.

Confident the tire chains would be the solution, I mounted the chains on the rear wheels after a little shoveling. Before reentering the cab, I shoveled away the snow in front of the truck. Once in the cab, I tried to go backward and forward to rock the truck into motion.

The narrow tires gradually made a short rutted path, but every time I tried to plow forward I got stuck and had to shovel excess snow not just in front, but also from under the truck. Very time- and energy-consuming.

I tried backing up the hill, but made no progress climbing the grade. Forward it was.

After repeatedly getting stuck and having to shovel excess

snow from under and in front of the truck, minimal progress had been made. I could see the sharp corner ahead and thought about taking a shortcut across the field to where I could see the other farmhouse. Finding no real ditch or fencing off the road-bed, I began walking a diagonal path across the field.

Fortunately, there wasn't any strong wind that day, so neither my legs or hands got cold from damp choppers or cotton jeans. Walking in knee-deep field snow, I sensed the snow had less crust to it than the roadbed. After maybe 100 feet of walking I turned and walked alongside my original footpath back to the truck. In walking this way, I hoped to lower the snow the Model A would have to buck against.

Bolstered with renewed confidence, I shoveled an exit path off the roadbed to the plowed field. The tire chains chattered as they grabbed bits of overturned clods. Slowly the truck came to the end of my footpath and forward progress stopped. The truck would not inch forward or backward without more shoveling and lead path making. Both my friend and I walked a forward leading path and back to the truck over and over as we slowly made progress across the field. It was taxing our energy reserve.

Not wanting to waste valuable time, we quickly ate what we had. Walking became trudging. Shoveling snow became more like shoveling cement. Climbing into the cab took required effort. Sitting in the cab's minimal heat felt good. To sit wasn't an option, though, because shivers came. To sit also wasn't an option, because I needed to get home before my parents.

Motivated, I labored exhausted and cold, with arm and leg muscles quivering. The normal reserve of stamina and drive had been called upon and vanished when I realized how low the sun was in the west. For the first time that day, a sense of desperation overcame me. Within an hour it would be absolutely dark.

It was then I noticed a glow from the distant farmhouse's nighttime yard light.

All day my decisions had been bad. The next decision had to be superior, and it was. Both of us began walking across the field toward the yard light. Fortunately, when we arrived at the farmhouse, we were warmly welcomed into the home. Without hesitation the farmer volunteered to pull us across the remaining distance with his powerful tractor. He and I went back to the truck.

The tractor groaned through the snowdrifts and pushed a path to the Model A. A short, stout chain was wrapped around the front axle. For the last time, the excess snow around and under the Model A was removed before I started the engine. As he slowly pulled away I assisted by driving the truck in first gear. Between the tractor's power and the truck's power, we traversed the field remaining without stopping.

The farmer was smiling, and I couldn't express enough appreciation. When I shut off the truck's engine and set the emergency brake, I realized the first stars of the evening sky were twinkling.

Though I desperately wanted to leave immediately to get home, we couldn't. While we were retrieving the truck, the housewife prepared a soup-and-sandwich meal for us. We were grateful as we ate and warmed our chilled bodies for the 30-mile ride back to Duluth.

Many times I wondered what they thought of us two boys. Would we have been assisted the same way by city-dwellers? I had no money to offer them—only sincere gratitude. Could we have perished that night? Absolutely.

The event, the people, and the outcome had a tremendous impact on me. Even today, where I live in a rural setting, my wife doesn't quite understand why I help people in need or turn down offerings of gratuities. Softly I say, "The Lord looks after me."

Under the yard light we scurried into the pickup. Headlights on! Moving with such ease, no chatter of tire chains clanking against the steel fenders, we rolled along on the farmer's driveway, a couple of hundred feet to the blacktop county road. No ice fishing today. We were southbound for home.

Only one mile down the road, the Model A began to slow. I pushed harder on the gas pedal, thinking my boot may have slipped off the pedal since much frozen snow and ice had accumulated on the floorboards while getting in and out of the truck. Finally, in frustration, I lifted my foot to reposition it on the gas pedal.

As soon as I lifted my foot, the Model A came to a stop.

I pushed in the clutch to keep the engine running. First, an odd, hot, burning odor was detected. Stopped with the engine running and headlights on, my mind raced with thoughts. What was wrong? Presently an engulfing blue color appeared to roll past us into the headlight beam.

Not knowing what to the rear of the truck could be the cause, I knew I had to get the Model A off the highway. While attempting to relocate the mid-floor-mounted gearshift lever from third gear to first gear in the dark cabin interior, my mittened hand accidentally bumped the emergency brake lever.

Shocked, I realized that in our haste to leave the farmhouse I had forgotten to release the emergency brake lever. Promptly I released the brake.

What would happen if I shifted to first gear and let out the clutch? Did I burn out some wheel bearings? Could something catch on fire? Will I be able to brake to stop? Driven by one overpowering thought—I have to get home before my parents—I put it in low gear and again headed home.

Quickly the odor and smoke were behind us. The truck stopped on command at the next intersection. All seemed well.

Before long, streetlights emerged ahead. First business was to drop off my friend who lived two blocks away from my home. It would have been nice to coast home and quietly slip the pickup into its parking space. But that not being an option, I drove next to the garage and parked the truck. The house had a few lights on, not many. And a small light was on in the garage.

Thinking the worst was about to come, I took a deep breath and prepared to tell the truth and accept the much-dreaded consequences.

My parents, who had just arrived at home, were in the midst of unpacking the car from their long day's trip. That may have helped, for when I told the truth—my day's plans, the intentions, and the near-disastrous side trip (I never mentioned the seized brakes)—they displayed only moderate displeasure. Not at all the much-anticipated anger and instant, stern behavioral consequences.

Nevertheless, I disappeared to my bedroom, studied, and went to bed thinking that the ax would surely fall tomorrow.

Fearing the worst, I joined the family for breakfast on Monday morning. We ate breakfast together seven days of the week.

I was actually looking forward to going to school that morning. Even though I tried to act normal at breakfast, I had nothing to chatter about. Nor did anyone else. Anxiously sitting in the quiet environment, I was perplexed that Sunday's fiasco never surfaced. Finished with breakfast, table cleared, dishes done, the next thing on my mind was an urgency to get to the school bus stop without any admonishment.

All day in school I was in a somber, studious mood. Focused, yet not focused on the academic tasks at hand, scenes from Sunday's stupidity vividly flashed across my memory's screen. Worst of all were the ever-present thoughts of what repercussions the ill-fated journey would have once I got home from basketball practice. An abundant nervous anxiety was within me all day.

During the evening, when the disastrous deed had not been broached, I began to think that my much-deserved punishment may have been self-imposed—the excessive reflective deliberation and scrutiny of my deeds. This, punctuated by my parents' silence, was more than adequate admonishment and penance.

Is this where I learned to stand on my own two feet and to tell the truth? If so, all the other learned experiences (even though they may have had tragic results) were minor compared to the life lesson of telling the truth.

Was the black Model A part of that valuable lesson? Absolutely.

10
Teenage Options

A piece of my childhood was behind me. The following spring I entered a new phase of my youthful years when I successfully passed both the written and behind-the-wheel portions of the driver's license exam.

When it came time for the behind-the-wheel exam, I used the family car. Satisfying the examination officer on the hills of Duluth with the family car, which had a manual transmission, was difficult enough. Prior to the actual exam, the examination officer does a vehicle safety inspection. Would the antique truck with only one standard taillight, one standard windshield wiper, no standard turn signals, and mechanical brakes have passed the vehicle inspection? It made no sense to test the system even though the pickup was my vehicle of choice.

Philosophy. Rural perspective. Independence. Now that I had my driver's license, what was my parents' philosophy regarding my usage of the Ford pickup truck? Would I be able to scoot about town to events with friends? What limits would be placed upon me regarding my desire to explore, camp, fish, hunt, and so on using the Model A? Was I expected to find a job to support my adventures?

Three considering factors influenced and ultimately shaped many of those decisions. First, both my parents were raised in rural settings. They had a sense of appreciation for the wonders of nature and a sense of pride in hard-working values. They may have questioned the amount of leisure time city youth had, and more so what they did with that time. As a result, a philosophy developed: It was better that I be camped on a lake at 10 p.m. than parked or hanging out in some alley at 10 p.m. Hence, many times in the following years, as encouragement to enjoy the outdoors, I was given gas money and groceries. At $0.25 per gallon, $2 went a long way.

Second, spending summers, weekends and free time in my childhood at the grandparents' homestead, surrounded by the vast freedom of rural areas, nurtured my enthusiasm to spend as much time as possible outdoors. In fact, in 1953, I was allowed to camp and fish for brook trout on famous streams along the North Shore of Lake Superior. A Duluth neighbor and retired fireman took me to the Baptism, Split Rock and Cascade rivers where I caught the speckled beauties on angleworms collected from our vegetable garden. Neat!

Later that summer, the Johansons (other neighbors), with their son, Bill, who was a year younger than me, asked me to accompany them on a 5-day lake trout fishing and camping trip to the Gunflint Trail. What an area! What a camping trip! What great fishing!

Overwhelmed with the experience, I was convinced that adventures in the outdoors were superior to any alley activities. This single episode with the Johansons impacted me for life. Career choices were made, seasonal property purchased, eventual permanent residence undertaken, and, most importantly, I met my beautiful wife.

The third factor that allowed me ample time over the next few years before college was self-employment and parental support. My ambitions and eagerness to work were rewarded when I was very young. As I referred to earlier, both sets of my grandparents lived in rural areas. I was fortunate that they wanted me to visit over the weekends during the school year.

Even on a retired farm, I found many chores that I enjoyed doing outdoors. One particular task was to erect snow fence in the fall and remove the snow fencing in the spring. It was a two-person task to lift into place and tie to wooden posts the slab snow fence. In either case, the fencing was placed on a wooden skid drag and pulled by either the Model A truck or a Ford 8N tractor. Great fun!

Much to my surprise, before returning home on Sunday, the grandfathers would pay me actual dollars. Wow! Every dollar I banked. Soon the following summers I was mowing yards for senior and some not-so-senior Duluth neighbors. I even got paid extra for hand trimming. My reputation grew for being able to mow grass on the steep hillside yards in Duluth.

During my high school years, the Model A truck transported the mower in the pickup box to 15 to 20 yards a week. After yard work, people asked me to wash windows and paint. I did whatever I could to earn and save a dollar. People were always good to me and understood when I explained I was going to take the truck and go camping for three days.

During my high school years my parents never suggested I get a "real" job, such as at the grocery store. Thus I was able to come and go (explore, camp and fish) through summer and still learn about employment responsibilities and savings. What a truly marvelous time in my life. Such sweet memories. And to think that little black truck was a reliable daily companion.

11

Truck Customizing

Accessorize! That is what Dad did to the Model A the summer I earned my driver's license. During this time, I was taught and participated in many mechanical rudiments. For starters, he replaced the standard Model A engine with a Model B engine. The Model B, which Ford Motor Company began manufacturing in 1932, had more horsepower, thus enabling a slightly higher highway traveling speed. When he finished the installation of the used engine, he reset the odometer to zero. Today, as I write this, the odometer reads 58,703 miles. No doubt those are mostly actual miles I myself put on the Model A. A huge share of those miles came on trips to and back from the Gunflint Trail, a minimum of 300 miles round-trip.

In addition to the B engine, he acquired a set of two Model B wheels. These rims allowed a wider tire to be mounted on the rim. These wider tires could support a bigger load, provide more tire surface on the road for both traction and flotation, and tended to be more durable and long-lasting. These tires were mounted on only the rear axle. The narrow, standard Model A tires remained on the front axle.

Flat tires could be a problem in those days, so he installed an additional spare-tire carrier in the right front fender. Since the original spare tire was mounted in the left front fender, the truck now carried two spare tires.

Of course, an axle jack for changing tires, and a lug nut wrench were always carried under the seat in the storage compartment. However, when mired in muck, an axle jack was insufficient in lifting ability and extremely hard to get in position to lift. Hence, a 3-foot-high lift jack with an extra handle was placed in the cab storage area behind the backrest cushion.

Ahead of its time. That is what I think today of the efficient homemade winch Dad made and mounted to the front bumper and between the two front fenders of the truck. The winch was installed to pull the truck out of a stuck position, which most often was a mud hole.

A 6-volt starter motor engaged the proper gearing to the cable spool. When the activation switch, mounted under the dash and energized by the truck battery, was pushed, the cable—secured to a tree or stump in front of the truck—tightened and slowly extracted the stuck vehicle. What further made this winch unique was not just its ability to draw the vehicle forward, but also backward. That is, if I realized it was futile to proceed ahead, I could pull the vehicle backward.

This was achieved by placing the cable over a pulley welded to the front bumper and then under the truck and finally secured to an immovable object behind the truck. Getting unstuck this way saved a lot of time that would have been spent jacking up the truck to place logs or other items under the wheels, over and over, until the truck was free or on solid ground. It also meant one person could free the vehicle by himself.

The winch was used often. It gave me the ability to explore more tote roads. It was simply ahead of its time—ahead of four-wheel drive and all-terrain vehicles.

Another extremely important accessory was a canoe rack.

Better lights, a winch and dual spare tires were added to the Model A.

How was I going to carry a canoe on such a vehicle? Towing a watercraft just wasn't an option. Besides, I didn't own a boat or a trailer. Nor did I own a canoe, but my mother's brother, Uncle Jim, left his 16-foot canvas-over-cedar-strip Brule River canoe at the farm when he moved to Montana years ago. It was mine to use. But imagine how perplexed I felt as a teenager trying to figure out how to carry a 16-foot canoe on a 4-foot truck box!

Perplexing for me—not a problem for a talented father. The total length of any Model A is approximately 12 feet, 6 inches. That means the canoe was 3 feet, 6 inches longer than the total length of the truck. Dad put his creative welding and drafting experience to work. He fabricated a removable canoe rack for both the front and the rear of the truck. Using variable diameters of steel pipe, he constructed a durable, removable front bracket that attached to the steel plate the winch was mounted on. The winch still remained usable.

Another removable canoe bracket was designed to fit in the rear stake pockets of the pickup box. Over the cross-bar on the rear bracket he placed a plastic pipe, which rolled while I struggled to position the canvas canoe. The plastic pipe also protected the wooden gunnels from marring.

These original canoe brackets were so well-designed they never needed modification for any canoe placed on them, such as the 17-foot Alumacraft canoe I purchased when I graduated from high school. Later, the same brackets proved valuable in transporting plywood, 21-foot lengths of galvanized water pipe, and 2-foot by 8-foot by 16-foot lumber when I built my first cabin on West Bearskin Lake on the Gunflint Trail.

It was time for an interior makeover. Needless to say, the hard use that came in the first 25 years of the truck's life had taken its toll. After removing the shredded interior door panels, we used them as patterns on durable tempered quarter-inch hardboard. Once cut, the panels fit perfectly. The panels were waterproofed and painted on both sides before being installed.

The ragged seat and back cushion were carefully separated from the springs and metal forms. We traced these patterns on heavy-duty naugahyde. Dad sewed the naugahyde, complete with piping, on his sturdy, table-mounted Singer sewing machine. After 58,703 miles of use, these look just as good as the day they were fabricated and installed. The interior was vastly improved.

Automobiles in the 1950s had radios powered by a 12-volt electrical system. The Model A was powered by a 6-volt electrical system. No 1950s automobile radio was compatible with a Model A. So when transistor radios became common, I tried listening to a transistor radio while traveling 40-45 mph along the north shore of Lake Superior, on my way to the Gunflint Trail.

It never worked. First, the electrical static from the Model A's electrical system interfered something terrible with the radio. Second, the engine noise was so loud that even with radio earplugs I couldn't detect much music. Finally, I was frequently out of the signal's range and received nothing but occasional radio skip over the airwaves. So much for entertainment.

Washboard gravel roads, engine vibration, and rough use caused ample metal fatigue on the Model A's fenders. Have you ever bent a piece of metal back and forth to break it off?

Dad's answer to fender metal fatigue cracks was to gas weld the cracks and leave a bit of excess iron to prevent further cracking on the surface of the fender. Most everyone knows how quickly bare iron rusts when exposed to the elements of nature. To prevent rusting, shortly after welding, the fenders of the Model A were prepped for painting. Basic Model A Fords were famous for their standard black paint.

Dad sprayed the body, which included running boards, fenders, radiator shell, hood, cab, and pickup box, with black paint on a Saturday in the family garage. The following week, after the fresh paint had dried, the Model A was moved outdoors, jacked up and placed on wooden blocks. My job was to remove all the wheels and dismount the tires in order for the wheel rims to be prepped, primed and painted. Dad chose an authentic production color—yellow—for the wheels.

Once the wheels were painted and tires remounted on the

rims and bolted onto the axle hubs, I couldn't wait to drive the Model A down the street to show it off. However, an extra touch was added to the paint job: yellow pinstriping. Wow, did the yellow pinstripe accent the hood, doors and pickup box!

The Model A now attracted much attention when I drove it. Why? Not just because it looked outstanding, but also because the Model A had long since disappeared from mainstream use on the byways of America.

Unique to the Model A pickup truck was an under-the-seat divided storage compartment. In one section, ample tools for repairs and spare parts were stashed. The spare parts included a timing gear, head gasket, spark plugs, points and condenser, electrical coil, engine oil, antifreeze, and an assortment of nuts and bolts. Of course, baling wire was always carried. In the second compartment emergency items were kept—things like an axe, waterproof matches, flashlight, rope, canvas, and an ice scraper.

Two noteworthy items were carried year-round: tire chains (two sets) and flares. A large set of chains were made for the wider Model B rear tires. These were the type that are still used today for travel in heavy snow conditions. The second set, called strap chains, were unique and are no longer in use today. Strap chains were used on rims that had spokes versus the all-steel or aluminum rims of today. They went on quick and easy. These were most often used to get you out of one bad spot, like, say, off a lake while ice fishing. The second item always carried were flares, sometimes called railroad flares. These were carried not for light or highway emergencies, but rather to ensure that a fire could be started under any conditions.

Noteworthy also to mention in the array of stuff under the seat was a sealed jar of 22 shells. Dad put these there, I believe, as a matter of old-time practice to carry extra emergency ammunition. However, unless it was hunting season, I never carried a gun while camping or fishing.

There was one very notable item Dad removed from under the seat: Jim Swanson's sawed-off single-shot break-action 12-gauge shotgun. I knew it was always there, wrapped in a heavy wool Army blanket. I never saw it used. All I know is that 50 years later, when I was helping Dad move out of the family house in Duluth, we found the sawed-off length of barrel. He gave the length of barrel to his longtime friend. Jim called the gun a keepsake.

12

Map Opens New Horizons

With the pickup in good-looking shape, I drove it to various antique car displays and in parades in several small towns in northern Minnesota and Wisconsin that summer. Often as incentive to participate and as a thank you, these small towns presented colorful metal plaques to participants. Someplace, I still have plaques from Ashland, Spooner, and Hayward, Wisconsin and from Grand Rapids, Cloquet, and Hibbing, Minnesota. While participating in a parade in Grand Marais, Minnesota, a Shold Lovaas Oil banner was hung on the passenger door.

Parades were fun, as I could leave early in the morning and return home to Duluth the same day. But I wanted to continue the tradition of exploring, camping, fishing and hunting in northern Minnesota. I had the support from my folks, especially my dad. After getting home from work on Friday night, he would tweak the Model A for a longer trip. He might remove the engine's oil pan to shim the connecting rods or maybe replace the sealant on the water pump. Before I left on a trip, often on Saturday morning, he would fill the 10-gallon gas tank, supply me with an extra 5 gallons of gas, give me $2 extra for an emergency, and ask me where I was going.

Before I set out exploring, I needed a better map than I could get free at the Standard Oil gas station or AAA. It was suggested that I inquire at a specialty store in downtown Duluth called A & E. It is there I purchased a fold-up map

Essential camping supplies — steel fishing pole, kerosene lantern, WWII one burner stove and map.

with an orange cover titled "Sportsman's and Tourist Map of the Minnesota Arrowhead."

The map contained Cook, Lake, and the east half of St. Louis County. It had many features: lakes, streams, roads, towns, campgrounds, forestry units, etc. On the cover, it declared, "Where hunting and fishing vacation dreams come true."

Today the map is frail. It has been repaired with Scotch tape, masking tape, and book-binding tape. All of these tapes have become brittle with age.

With the aid of this map and the Model A truck, I visited areas that now lie within the BWCAW. Much later in life, I used this map to research and locate abandoned fire towers, resorts, mine sites, and both private and government-owned cabins in the BWCAW. Even Dorothy Molter's property is identified on this artifact. I call it, simply, the orange map.

One of my favorite places to explore in the summer with the aid of the map was the area west, north, and east of Kawishiwi Lake. Often I would pitch a floorless canvas tent on the edge of Kawishiwi Lake. Loons called during the night, fish could be heard jumping, and soft breezes whispered in the tall pines.

Back then, many, many lakes had picnic tables at popular campsites provided by the USFS as part of the Superior National Forest recreational plan. Campers, like me, appreciated the tables. If the weather was nice, it was common to leave one's food box or pack on the picnic table overnight or even through the next day while fishing. I never had a bear try to get at my food until many years later, while camping at a designated site within the BWCAW.

For campers of that earlier era, a Coleman lantern fueled by white gas would provide supplementary evening light. I disliked them because for some reason the fragile mantle would often break on me during transport. They also emitted a loud hissing sound, which took away from the magnificent sounds of a north woods night.

When I shared this problem with my grandfather, he promptly retrieved from his garage a metal Dietz #2 Blizzard kerosene lantern, complete with a heavy-duty glass chimney.

The warm yellow light it dispensed was more than adequate for my needs. It required very little fuel. If I knew I would be portaging, I poured the fuel into a container; otherwise the fuel could spill if the lantern tipped over. Several evenings while camping, I did the dinner dishes on a picnic table using the lantern's light. Today I still cherish the Dietz lantern—especially when we lose electrical power during a storm.

That fall, late in October, over a four-day break from school, I made a solo hunting trip to the Kawishiwi Lake area. The weather was glorious for late October—frosty mornings followed by 40-degree flannel-shirt sunshine in the afternoons. There may have been several reasons why I encountered so few other hunters: extreme remoteness, the lateness of the season, or other hunting-location options. Regardless, I had the area to myself.

With the Model A I chugged along every tote road or side trail until I came to its end, when I would turn around and retrace my incoming route. At times, without leaves on the deciduous trees, I came upon spectacular vistas. Often I had to refer to a compass and my sportsman's map to identify a fire lookout tower off in the distance.

Mid-afternoon on Saturday was particularly memorable. With the pickup I had followed a trail in search of grouse. The trail was growing narrower because of encroaching brush from both sides. Finally, I made a decision to turn around.

In the process of turning around, I glanced out the passenger window and spotted three grouse standing in line on a log with their heads up, looking at the truck—a strange black alien in their woods.

Excitedly I straightened out the truck on the trail and got out to see if the grouse were still on the log. Much to my surprise, they were.

Rapidly I put one .410 shell in the gun's chamber and aimed

at the head of the middle grouse, hoping that the shot pattern would scatter enough to kill the other two grouse. Kaboom! When I lowered the gun, three grouse were flapping on the ground.

I did my best golden-retriever move and gathered them up. Wow! Three grouse with one shot! That made up for a couple of wing shots I had missed earlier that day. Never have I duplicated that feat. Could the Model A have mesmerized the three grouse?

13

Thin Ice

Sometime between summer and Thanksgiving, I managed to build my fish house. It cost me very little, as Grandpa, who had built his own years before, supplied the materials and construction expertise. Uncle Kenny fabricated a small wood-burning stove out of heavy plate iron as a source of heat. It outlasted any light tin wood stove one could buy. At that time, portable propane heaters were not available.

Now I could go ice fishing on my own in my own house. The fish house was stored at Grandpa's, just a couple of miles from the excellent northern pike lake.

Just a side note—today the Minnesota DNR (Department of Natural Resources) issues an electronic paper decal to adhere to a fish house. Do you remember the round aluminum disks with a number pressed into the metal the DNR issued years ago?

That November, even during deer season, I cherished the cold temperatures that would cause the lakes to freeze over with ice eventually. Prior to Thanksgiving, weather bulletins reported that area lakes had frozen over for the season and the first ice fishermen were venturing out onto the lakes. With that good news and no school, I scripted a plan for the Friday after Thanksgiving to tow the fish house to Lake Nichols.

Turkey sandwiches on homemade buns were made the night before for Friday's lunch. Two inches of snow was forecast overnight. Last-minute fishing tackle and winter clothes were piled in the Model A to enable a rapid sunrise departure from Duluth.

Once again this was a solo venture, as the other men had to report to work. White rivers of snow driven by a north wind flowed across the blacktop as I made the 30-mile drive to Grandpa's home. Since I arrived well before 8 a.m., he was there to give me my first lesson on how to tie the fish house behind the truck so it would tow and not zigzag off to one side or the other. Before leaving for the lake, he presented me with a sleek, hand-crafted, deadly metal spear and three hand-carved, weighted wooden decoys. (Now I recognize how talented and capable the Olsons were at making things.)

Fresh snow was perfect for towing the fish house on the gravel road. In 15 minutes I reached the public access to the lake. Much to my surprise, tall, light brown grass and cattails stood on the lakeshore. From inside the truck's cab, I realized no one had ventured onto the white expanse covering the lake.

At first I was hesitant to continue, not knowing if I could get the 6-foot by 6-foot fish house through the tall grass and cattails. Since the snow wasn't deep in the vegetation and knowing I had tire chains under the seat, along with a shovel, I was confident about getting through the dry plants. Besides, the thought of being the first on the lake enabled me to claim a choice fishing location along the edge of the weed bed off the island where Grandpa had chosen to place his fish house many years in a row. There was a lot of competition among fish house owners for this "hot spot."

The bumper of the Model A pushed the grass and cattails

down. Soft, fluffy cattail duff filled the air in front of the windshield as the truck cautiously eased through the slender cattail blades. Effortlessly, with fish house in tow, the truck glided across the level white expanse to the island. Nearing the island, I drove in a small circle so the truck was pointed toward the public access for easy egress. From memory I judged the distance and location of the weed bed from the island and rolled to a stop.

How proud I was of the Model A for pulling the fish house through the grass and across the lake with such fluidity. How proud I was of my fish house sitting on the lake in a light snowfall. How good I felt being outdoors without a cabin in sight or another person around. How excited I was when, after a single jab to the ice with an ice chisel, I discovered the ice thickness to be only 2-3 inches!

Make that "terrified." Numb with fear, frozen to the spot, thoughts of the truck and myself going through the ice paralyzed my body actions. With great care I eased the chisel into the box of the truck, untied the fish house, and with graceful, feather-light movements reentered the cab. With great smoothness I started and coaxed the truck in a forward motion directly to the public access. Relieved to be on solid land, my legs quivered when I got out of the truck.

After rationalizing and gathering confidence, I did walk out to the fish house with my lunch and other fishing paraphernalia. The rest of the day, thoughts of what could have happened ran through my mind repeatedly. Later I realized that both Grandpa and Dad thought I was going to tow the fish house to the lake, not onto the lake.

Bob with large
northern and his
Model A.

Oh yes, I did bring home fresh fish for supper. Never did I share this frightening episode with anyone. It was nothing to brag about. A Model A pickup weighs less than 1,000 pounds, which is about a quarter the weight of a full-size modern pickup.

14

Ingenuity Born

Eventually winter's icy grip eroded. Soon, the number of watercraft towed behind vehicles on the highway forecasted great interest by anglers testing fishing equipment before the walleye opener. My simple equipment—canvas canoe, paddle, tent, kerosene lantern, and mess kit—needed no spring testing. What I needed was a destination. A lake.

Poring over my Sportsman map and consulting DNR references, Isabella Lake received high recommendations for an opening-weekend walleye fishing and camping escapade. Pumped with youthful energy, as soon as I got home from school on Friday afternoon I headed north for Isabella Lake.

The Model A had been prepped for the sojourn days before. Thursday evening, the canoe was lashed on the overhead brackets and all non-food supplies positioned in the box under a canvas.

Being mid-May, the two-hour-plus trip was completed with ample daylight. Caravans of heavy traffic were encountered on Highway 61. At that time, the four-lane express between Duluth and Two Harbors didn't exist.

Was the short black Model A truck loaded with a 17-foot canvas canoe conspicuous in the caravan? Probably not, as many other vehicles, from station wagons and sedans to pickups, hauled boat trailers, pop-up camping trailers, fifth-wheelers, and multi-level canoe trailers toward northerly destinations. Often through the years when I met an oncoming

Minnesota Highway Patrol vehicle, I pondered the officer's thoughts as he passed my antiquated transportation.

It is a fact that I never exceeded the speed limit on the highway. I couldn't. The Model A had a very limited ability. As a result, passing on the highway wasn't an option either.

For many reasons, this walleye opener was special. This year I joined the rush north to experience an opener on my own. Of course, I wanted to hook numerous fish, maybe even a monster, but more important to me was seeking out a remote location. Already in my youth I had experienced long waiting lines at boat accesses, fishing boats loaded with anglers so close together lines and lures became tangled, and even shoulder-to-shoulder angling from bridges over open water many feet below. My sense of aesthetic fishing had already been raised. No longer could I value and appreciate nature under crowded circumstances.

Most everything at Isabella Lake met my approval: its remoteness, lack of crowds, clean environment, excellent water quality, and relatively easy access. With so many attributes, there was still the ultimate question: Could I catch fish from these waters?

At the campsite, the tailgate of the Model A served as my picnic table. The early-morning sunshine served up warmth as I ate an easy breakfast of cold cereal and a jelly sandwich. In the early light of dawn, I struggled, as I always did, getting the heavy canvas canoe off the rack and beached at the rocky edge of the lake. With camping gear stowed in the truck and fishing lures stowed onboard the canoe, I pushed quietly away from shore. Afloat in a calm cove, my instincts sensed the marvels of the serene lake. Whirligigs and water striders skittered on the surface. Crayfish and other insect larvae scudded among the pebbles under the water. Miniature snails clung to sub-surface sticks. Newly hatched mosquitoes danced on and off the liquid surface of the lake. Mating and territorial calls of arriving migratory birds issued from the vibrant, fresh, fragrant forest of both coniferous and deciduous species. A slight tinge of soft green of the deciduous buds about to burst open in warm southerly breezes presaged the arriving summer. It was a marvelous spring walleye opener. Need I catch fish? I felt spiritually and emotionally refreshed.

Until I sneezed, with a racket that interrupted the peaceful scene like a blaring foghorn on the shores of Lake Superior. Needing to wipe the effluent mess from under my nose, I reached for my massive red handkerchief from one of my rear jeans pockets. Struggling to extract the balled-up hanky from the tight pocket without overturning the canoe, I gave a final, mighty yank. Ah, success! The hanky was in hand. But what was that subtle, strange noise I had detected at the side of the canoe behind me ?

Shock raced through my mind as I realized that when I pulled out the hanky, so had I ejected the only ignition key I had to the Model A.

It was already too late—and the water much too deep—to make a desperate one-handed lunge for the key. In the transparent water, the bright brass key and chain reflected the rays of morning sunlight until they vanished from sight forever.

Moments elapsed. My mind was blank. Not even a curse came from my lips. Instantly my interest in fishing waned. All the beauty and glory that seconds ago surrounded me dissolved. Options skipped across my brain. Retrieval just didn't seem feasible without scuba equipment. Phone service was 20-25 miles away, maybe. Walking and hitchhiking to somewhere was a long shot, but possible. Maybe another angler would arrive today and either give me a ride or call Duluth when they got back to civilization. Or I could just wait enough days for my folks or a rescue team to come when I didn't return to Duluth on Sunday night.

Disconsolate, I returned to the Model A and sat dejected and lonely on the running board. It would do no good to cry or curse. This was my doing and where I had wanted to be. Why, I had even wished for isolation and a lack of fellow anglers competing for a niche on the lake.

Fifteen minutes. Thirty minutes. Time elapsed like sand through a giant hourglass as I pondered the possibilities.

If I could overcome this calamity on my own, how much increased trust and independence would I earn in my parents' eyes? That notion, that concept, kept me motivated to pursue every hypothesis. Now I perceived my dilemma wasn't life-threatening. Stamina and strength from positive thoughts brought new notions and suppositions to my predicament. Abruptly, a plausible, intelligent idea burst to the forefront. What would happen if I bypassed the ignition switch?

After all, all a key does is complete an electrical circuit. Now this was a significant scheme. At first I believed I would have to smash the metal capsule that held the key. That would require removing from the dashboard the metal case—not easy. Being up and moving on my feet, studying the dashboard, and

88

raising both sides of the hood helped me visualize a complete switch assembly. I had seen extra switch assemblies with keys hanging in Grandpa's garage.

Bingo! Instantly I realized how to bypass the ignition switch. On the firewall under the hood, a fiber block with ignition switch wires held the solution. All I had to do was connect one terminal end to the other terminal end on the engine side with, preferably, a metal wire.

Wire was not a problem, nor were tools. Thankfully, a Model A ignition switch was extremely simple. I found a wire and put it in place. No electrical sparks.

Very confident, I climbed aboard, set the controls, and stepped on the floor starter switch. After a couple of revolutions the engine roared to life.

Total elation overcame me. I passed the test. Brimming

Upgraded lights and a homemade winch were helpful when exploring the back country.

with pride, I let the engine idle, not daring to shut it off. Wait a minute! How could I shut it off ? I had to load up the canoe and gear and go home. Wait another minute—did I have to go home? This was the walleye opener. If I could figure out how to start the Model A, surely I could figure out how to shut it off and restart it at will.

More self-assured than I ever felt before, after twice starting and stopping the Model A, I resumed fishing after a two-and-a-half-hour delay. From that day forward, a spare key was always carried on board every vehicle I owned. Incidentally, I caught and released many fish on an orange flat fish lure the remainder of the weekend.

I gained experience that walleye-opener weekend, but probably more significant was my growth in self-esteem, thanks to the simplicity of a Model A pickup.

15

Influenced

On the highway early that spring, I observed several vehicles transporting resplendent, shining aluminum canoes. These lightweight, durable watercraft were growing in popularity. They were economical and offered years of maintenance-free service. These solid attributes lured me to compare two brands: Grumman and Alumacraft. The 17-foot Grumman canoe was an elegantly designed craft with beautiful workmanship, which included tapered, flush rivet heads throughout its construction. The 17-foot Alumacraft, on the other hand, was a machined masterpiece. It featured durable gunnels and gunnel end caps, which bode well for rocky portaging.

Three items influenced me to purchase the Alumacraft canoe: the portaging yoke that came standard, the price, and the name of the 17- foot model.

A canoe is portaged overturned above one's head on shoulders. Shouldn't a portaging yoke be standard equipment? I thought so. As for price, cigar-smoking Al Haglin from Haglin Marine in Superior, Wisconsin offered me a 17-foot canoe for $200. Sold! The competitors were nearly a hundred dollars more. Finally, the model's name, "Quetico," said it all. The Quetico, a canoeist's paradise, was a fabulous advertising product name suggesting both adventure and wilderness. In late May, the olive green canvas canoe was put in indoor storage. Meanwhile, the Quetico 17 LT is still in service after 50 years.

Rain or shine, it didn't matter; the Model A and the aluminum canoe became inseparable. That summer the canoe never came off the Model A's canoe rack unless it was at a body of water.

I made many memorable trips up the North Shore of Lake Superior to try fishing inland lakes. One trip was a total washout. Literally. Late one afternoon, a thunderstorm threatened, sending me to seek shelter in the cab of the Model A. Fortunately I was able to secure the canoe overhead on the rack before the deluge of rain descended. With the tumultuous storm came wind that took down tree limbs by the dozens.

When the heavy rain didn't cease, good judgment told me I better get to a better, graveled road since I was two or more miles on a narrow, overgrown trail that led to this remote lake. Luckily, no downed trees, lowland, or rain-swollen creek impeded my progress to the gravel road.

My fate changed a few miles from my campground destination. The torrential rain continued, raising water levels that flooded the road in the lowlands. With care I drove the Model A through water that came up to the running boards. Then, with much apprehension, I approached a swollen river. The speed and zest with which the wide river rolled past promised serious consequences should I venture forward.

Losing daylight, I drove in reverse through the floodwater until I reached high ground, where I turned around to head in the opposite direction. Travel in this direction was similarly treacherous. In addition to portions of the road being underwater, the roadbed was becoming increasingly soft, almost mushy. Could the shoulders of the road give way and suck the

Model A into a quagmire?

That certainly felt possible given the way the steering wheel pulled, so I maintained a steady course, straddling the center of the road in second gear. Glad to finally reach some high ground in the near-darkness, I paused in the dead center of the road to read my tourist map by flashlight. I dared not to shut off the Model A's engine in the ever-continuing rain. I surmised from the map that I was anywhere from 10 to 15 miles to the Sawbill Trail, a major artery that led to safety and Highway 61.

Maybe it would have been better to sit in the dark in the cab of the Model A in the absolute center of some nameless road, but an uneasy fear of being stranded prodded me to continue.

At spots with even the slightest grade, torrents of rain had washed gullies in the roadbed and strewn boulders as the glaciers had ages ago. After slow, deliberate progress, I paused at a... driveway?

A faint but steady glow appeared through the sheets of rain. Suddenly, in a timely flash of lightening, a small building materialized and swiftly vanished, I needed directions on where I was, and yes, I was feeling apprehensive. So, with map in hand, I left the Model A running with the weak headlights on, dashed to the door and knocked.

That set off the dog. Not one person, but a family of five— two adults and three children under 10—warily answered the knock. Hastily I explained that I needed directions as a result of the storm and road conditions.

The father welcomed me into the crowded mudroom with

a kerosene lantern in hand. Many fair faces gathered and peered at the wet map and me. The father identified my location on the map and gave directions. The sight of faces, the warm, dry room and the help lifted my spirits.

As I was folding the map into its orange case before departing, the father asked if I was alone. Was he going to ask me to stay? Quickly I replied yes, I was alone, and thanked them very much.

I had stopped for directions and for assurance, but I came away with a newly discovered appreciation for a different way of life. I had never lived in a house without electricity, running water, central heat, and toilets. Here was a family living the way both my parents had been raised.

After that brief encounter with that family, I sensed relief. The need to get out to safety didn't push me. Down the road, I found what appeared to be a high wide-open area where, for the first time in probably four hours, I turned the ignition switch to "off." Here, in the cab, I would make do until morning. After a few tidbits from the food pack, I made a pillow out of a spare jacket and a small canvas for cover and quickly fell asleep to the sound of the rain striking the metal roof of the Model A cab and the 17-foot canoe overhead.

When I returned home, I shared my trip experiences, of course, and I had questions galore for both parents. Each explained the daily chores they were expected to do and the lifestyle they had had as children raised in rural settings. Do you ever think about the changes you've seen in your lifetime?

Part 2: Gunflint Years
1
Bound for Gunflint

By midsummer of 1959, it was apparent to my parents that each adventurous outing took me further and further north. So when I broached the subject of traveling to the Gunflint Trail, they were not surprised.

Up to this point, most of my camping trips had been made to destinations within day-trip distance of Duluth. However, this was a different story. Traveling 150 to 200 miles one-way to the Gunflint Trail would require considerable time in a Model A. What would happen should I have vehicle problems? This was just one of the many questions I pondered. Aware of potential concerns, I asked permission from my parents to make the journey rather than telling them where I was going.

At their suggestion, I approached my friend Bill Johanson's parents to see if Bill could accompany me. Bill's parents were delighted. For further support, they planned to travel to the area two days behind our departure and stay at the same campground. That worked for all parties. By the end of summer, Bill and I made our first unsupported trip to the Gunflint. The following summer, I made solo trips routinely.

The Johansons always camped at the Flour Lake campground when they visited the Gunflint Trail. Thus it was determined Bill and I would camp there, too. Besides, Mrs. Johanson promised fresh-baked goodies and delicious meals when she

Loaded for trip to the Gunflint, note outboard on sideboard.

arrived.

Preparation for our initial trip north was easy. I always had my camping gear ready, the Model A got routine maintenance following any extended use, and our mothers joined forces to provide meals.

On our very first trip to the Gunflint, two traditions commenced: Dairy Queen and Erickson gas. These traditions lasted for years, even on my numerous solo trips. Both Bill and I loved ice cream, so it became a tradition to stop at the Two Harbors Dairy Queen for our favorite treat. Since our top speed was 45 mph, which even back then was considered slow, we always purchased the largest shake offered, hoping it would break up the traveling monotony and maybe, just maybe, last until we got to Grand Marais. (Of course, the cool treat never lasted that long.)

Once we reached Grand Marais, the second tradition was to fill up with gas at the Erickson (now Holiday) gas station. The gas station offered many of the latest conveniences: multiple gas pumps for quick in-and-out service, ample maneuvering space if trailering, last-minute convenience items ranging from bullets to boots, and a helpful and congenial owner, Mike Quaife.

Whether Mike was pumping gas, stocking shelves, or behind the checkout counter, he always had kind words, good advice and a smile. Maybe he always recognized me afterward because I fueled up my outdated black truck with yellow wheels and a canoe overhead. I still remember the look on his face when I told him I was from Duluth. I was never sure what he thought of my vehicle of choice. Even now, some 50 years later, when I see Mike around Cook County, his smile and warm greeting are genuine.

With Mike's advice on this initial Gunflint journey, I purchased a minnow-like Rebel Rapala lure. This durable black-over-silver floating plastic lure, complete with two treble hooks, was irresistible to the smallmouth bass on Flour Lake. This lure still has a favorite spot in my tackle box, even though it is minus some black paint from numerous vicious strikes from the fish on the Gunflint Trail.

No doubt when Bill's parents arrived a couple days later they were glad to see us safe. They prepared us a generous dinner with fresh fish. Around the campfire that evening, they discussed lake trout fishing plans for the next two days. Behind their 1952 two-tone green Dodge pickup they towed a 12-foot boat powered by a blue 5 HP Evinrude outboard motor. With all of the excellent trout lakes in the immediate area— Clearwater, West Pike, Mountain, West Bearskin, Duncan, Daniels and Rose—it was decided we could keep in contact with each other if we fished a small lake. Daniels Lake, down an old railroad grade, it was to be.

By nine o'clock the following morning we broke camp and with both vehicles headed down the road. At Clearwater Lodge, Mr. Johanson (in the lead) turned onto the railroad grade, which resembled a tote trail only inches above the surrounding swamp. This was complete with overhanging brush and limbs. Bill suggested I stay a ways back from the trailered boat in case the Dodge and trailer got mired in one of the mud holes.

Cautiously we advanced, occasionally either bouncing up and over railroad cross ties forced up by frost over the past 30 years (the General Logging Railroad had a brief existence in the area) or a sudden drop where a cross tie had been removed. The bed of the railroad grade under the Model A felt fairly firm until Bill said, "This is it!"

Ahead of us, the boat trailer disappeared in the mud behind the Dodge. The 12-foot boat appeared to glide along behind the truck, cutting a small wake in the mud, with the Evinrude's prop out of sight on the transom. With Bill's encouraging words ("They made it though the worst hole, it's our turn"), I nudged the black—soon to be brown—Model A forward.

Short, old blocks of logs sticking out of a quagmire in all directions told a story of an unsuccessful crossing attempt by somebody before us. Quickly I thought about being able to use the bumper-mounted winch should we get mired in the sinkhole, but only spindly alder surrounded the area—nothing strong or sturdy enough to anchor the winch. Across the 200-foot stretch, the narrow rubber front tires tracked in Mr.

Johanson's rut. The entire Model A veered sideways and one rear tire sank into a hole once filled with short wood chunks, yet our progress continued thanks to the truck's high clearance and the lack of a boat or trailer dragging behind. (Not too many years later, my grandfather accompanied me to the same area of the Gunflint Trail. When the fishing was slow or the winds too strong to be on a lake, we hauled many loads of rock in the box of the pickup and shored up the worst area on that road. We also cleared overhanging brush from the trail).

After the "worst," according to Bill, the last half-mile of railroad grade was good going. The railroad grade followed the south shore to the east end of Daniels and then north to the international border at Rose Lake. Along the narrow three miles or so of abandoned railroad grade from Clearwater Lodge to Rose Lake, it was explained to me, there were only two places to turn a vehicle around. The first was one and a quarter miles from the lodge where the railroad grade emerges from the swamp and meets Daniels Lake. At this site, the Johansons had to disconnect and jockey the boat trailer out of the way while they squeezed the Dodge into the turnaround, pull out onto the grade, and back north on the grade far enough that the Model A could do the same. We hoped no other vehicles came in while we were out fishing.

The typical early-summer morning calm was giving away to high, dark cumulous clouds and an increasing west wind. The plan was to fish the deep water on the west end along the steep rock wall. The Johansons would fish from the boat, Bill and I from the canoe. With fishing poles, tackle, landing net, lunches, and, most importantly, sucker minnows aboard each watercraft, we pushed off. The Evinrude pushed the light boat and occupants westward with ease while Bill and I pulled hard on the paddles, heading into the steadily increasing wind.

By the time Bill and I reached the west end of the lake, Bill's parents were already fishing. Their preferred technique was to drift across the deep, open expanse, suspending their bait off the bottom. Once they had completed the quarter- to half-mile drift, they would reel up, start the outboard, go back to the base of the rock cliff, and set adrift again.

With the wind growing steadily and upon the recommendation from Bill's dad, Bill and I paddled slowly in the lee of wind along the base of the cliff in 80 feet of water. It was thought that this approach would conserve our energy. Our fishing technique was similar to the successful technique used by Bill's parents.

We attached a frisky sucker minnow to a single hook, which followed one silver spinner about the size of a nickel. Attached three feet ahead of the bait and lure on a drop line was a quarter-ounce sinker. We paddled very slowly, the sinker dropped to or just above the bottom. The sucker minnow swam freely behind the flashing spinner. Every hundred feet or so, we would raise or drop our line, giving a vertical swimming motion to the bait. The key to success was paddling slowly in order to keep the bait within three feet of the bottom and the feeding zone. When the fish were aggressive they would set the hook themselves. Less-aggressive fish simply bit the tail off the sucker, often tearing the sucker off the hook. It was a simple, successful technique that we employed for years to come.

However, on this particular day, the fish didn't cooperate. Strong winds produced whitecaps. Both our energy and enthusiasm to struggle against the wind and the fish waned. By early afternoon, it felt good to stretch our legs and weary shoulders back at the launch site.

After turning over a few rocks on the shore, Bill and I became restless and eager for more adventure. Apparently, years ago, Bill's dad had been to Rose Lake via the railroad grade. He whetted our adventurous spirits by telling us about an old elevated wooden water tower for steam engines at the end of the tracks, a sand beach on Rose Lake, and an international stream that stretched for a mile before approaching Rose Lake. The stream was actually the international border between Canada and the United States.

Wow! Quickly we shuffled trucks at the launch site, boarded the Model A, and chugged along the very edge of Daniels Lake bound for Rose Lake. After two miles, we arrived at Rose Lake and the only place along the railroad grade to turn around the Model A.

The waves pounded the sand beach, first pushing grains of sand toward the vegetation line and then allowing the multicolor particles to roll back toward the clear depths of the border lake.

It wasn't long before Bill discovered the wooden remnants of the water tower. Young ash trees had sprouted all around the dilapidated site. Fortunately I was able to discover a significant piece of iron. Later, my grandfather, who worked his entire life on the railroad near Duluth, identified it as the maul head used to drive railroad spikes into the railroad cross ties to hold the rail tracks in place. Both Bill and I found and kept a half-dozen railroad spikes, which we later learned were used on lightweight iron rail used in bush country.

Before we left Rose Lake, we walked the sandy beach into Canada. In the northeast corner of the lake, past the high diabase bluff, we found remnants of a Canadian trail, which we followed into the pine forest for blocks until it began to ascend a steep grade. We climbed higher and higher until we reached the apex of the magnificent ancient rock formation. From this vantage point, numerous American and Canadian lakes appeared before us.

We carried no map, but later studied a topographic map. Parts of several Canadian lakes were identified: 20-mile-long Arrow Lake and Baker Lake. Five international lakes stretched both east and west: Rove/Watap, Rose, South, North and Gunflint. The American lakes included Clearwater and Daniels.

In the warm west wind, Bill and I sat and witnessed a bald eagle glide on the air currents below us, above the tops of the 200-year-old white pines. The wind through the pines created a roar. However, from the rock precipice upon which we stood, nearly no significant swaying motion could be detected.

On both Rose and Arrow lakes, the afternoon sun's light reflected off the liquid surface. Each of the many whitecaps created by the friction of wind sparkled like a diamond. Four hundred feet below us lay a vast and varied blue velvet showcase sprinkled with thousands of precious gems, enhanced by the solar rays and surrounded by an undulating green carpet.

Reluctantly Bill and I descended the peak and returned to the black Model A under the canopy of green. On the rail grade, the Model A flushed a very young covey of ruffed grouse. Some fledglings flew into the slender branches of alder along the international stream. Others scattered under the palm-size leaves of the thimbleberry plants. The Model A, unlike a well-trained retriever, didn't pursue a single grouse for its master. Instead it hesitated briefly for its occupants to deliberate the whereabouts of these year-round residents of the Gunflint Trail.

Yes, the Johansons did go fishing that afternoon while Bill and I explored. They caught one very nice lake trout, which Mrs. Johanson broiled over an open fire at the Flour Lake campsite. That evening, while enjoying the succulent trout, I was already internally contemplating and planning further trips to the Gunflint. The Model A may have been slow on the highway, but it excelled in the hinterlands of the Gunflint Trail. In the years to come, I enjoyed many adventures throughout the Gunflint Trail region. So did friends and family, especially my dad and grandfather, Alfred Olson, who spent many years traveling via the Model A pickup to the Gunflint Trail. Eventually I built both a seasonal cabin on West Bearskin Lake and a permanent residence on Clearwater Lake.

That same summer, Bill and I made two more exploring and fishing trips to the Gunflint, camping and fishing different lakes each time. We always caught fish for supper. By Labor Day I was confident I could travel to the Gunflint by myself. With my parents' permission, I headed to the northernmost reaches of Minnesota at the end of the Gunflint Trail in the 1930 truck, canoe overhead, for a four-day solo adventure.

I wasn't into portaging the canoe yet. Why should I, when

I could drive to so many lakes and launch my canoe ? But I did learn a couple of significant things on this excursion. First, a 17-foot canoe is difficult to maneuver by yourself in moderate winds, even if loaded with camping gear. Second, due to windy conditions, I quickly acquired a respect for safety on big lakes and, conversely, an appreciation for small lakes. The lee side of the islands on Saganaga and Seagull were a godsend I shall never forget. At the conclusion of this trip, I reluctantly put away my fishing equipment and began another year of schooling.

2
Beginning Solo Trips

High school was good. I made the football team as a sophomore. Team practice was immediately after school let out. Occasionally I would drive the pickup to school when practice was scheduled to last extra long. The truck attracted much gawking and created quite a stir in the school parking lot, where it sat next to '56 Chevys and Fords. The '56 Chevys and Fords were clad with chrome and pairs of fuzzy dice that hung from the chrome rear-view mirror. The only chrome on the Model A pickup was the carburetor choke knob. And, yes, the pickup had a black rectangular rear-view mirror, complete with a dangling grouse feather.

The responsibilities of school and football changed my carefree autumn attitude somewhat. Autumn grouse hunting did happen, but I had to check the calendar. Often to go hunting was a decision made on a Saturday or Sunday if the weather cooperated. Finally, after five weeks of school and Friday night football games, a four-day hiatus of school occurred. For sure I was going grouse hunting on the Gunflint.

This was okay with my parents, as they had trust in my judgment. My dad could not take time off from work during the week to accompany me. He, too, had work-related responsibilities. He also had confidence in my abilities to adjust to late October northern Minnesota camping. Once again he filled the 10-gallon Model A gas tank and supplied me with a full extra five-gallon gas can for reserve, as he usually would do before my departure.

Focusing on schoolwork Monday through Wednesday was difficult that week, to say the least. Upon getting home from school on Wednesday, I departed rapidly for the Gunflint. All the camping supplies and food were in the rear box of the pickup, except my supper, which was more like a lunch; I carried that in the cab of the truck. Since the Two Harbors Dairy Queen was closed by late October, I could eat my supper-lunch after leaving Two Harbors and before Silver Bay to help pass the time while motoring north on Highway 61.

Would I make Grand Marais before nightfall? I doubted it. Between Silver Bay and Grand Marais I entertained myself by doing my best rendition of Elvis Presley's "You Ain't Nothing But a Hound Dog," thinking it had something to do with hunting. Boy was I naïve!

As I remember it, there were not many hunters in the woods compared to today. Maybe because it was late October. Maybe because I was so far north. Whatever the reason, the region was void of humanity, and I loved it.

I didn't stay at an established campground, as they were closed. Late in the afternoon, I would set up a tent at the end of a tote road, such as Finn Lake Road, Rib Lake Trail, or one of the many South Lake trails.

Surprisingly, grouse were not overly abundant as they had been the previous summer. I surmised it was primarily because it was so late in the season. The grouse had scattered to winter habitat. Small ponds remained frozen over all day. Surely if snow fell now it would remain on the ground until spring.

Gunflint Trail bound with cedar strip canoe.

Five days, four nights. All the deciduous leaves had fallen. The fallen leaves on the frosty boreal earth lay shriveled and coffee-colored. Even the gilded needles of the tamaracks lay on the ground, waiting for the first snow.

Early Thursday morning, I found myself on a maze of logging roads off what I now call the old Greenwood Road. More than once, the Model A and I forded both small creeks and moderate-size creeks and streams. Occasionally, if a grouse was spotted well ahead on the muddy, rutted trail, it would hasten for the bush—either on foot or by flight. There were so many tote roads I could not drive them all. After lunch I reversed my path back to the blacktop of the Gunflint Trail. Was I going north or west? Whatever. It was in the opposite direction of the brown forest sign with yellow lettering, which pointed to Grand Marais. Along the blacktop trail, I soon passed the famous ladder signs telling distances to the resorts along the Gunflint Trail. Over the weekend I drove into many of the resorts. Most were closed for the season.

Thursday afternoon found me traversing the Lima Grade to Twin Lakes. I had crossed a stretch of water where the water could have entered the cab if I had opened the door. Little did I know I would have to drive through that stretch of water again until the road sort of dead-ended at Trestle Pine Lake.

The trestle that spanned the narrows of Trestle Pine Lake was long gone. I did not look forward to retracing my route through the deep-water slough to get out to the Gunflint. Fortunately, I made it across the swamp.

My adventures weren't over yet. My map showed a trail to Swan Lake. This was really dicey.

Wisely, I turned around. Why, that trail literally ran through a muskeg swamp, which wouldn't hold my weight when I ventured to walk on it. God must have been looking over my shoulder that afternoon. Later, sitting around a diminutive evening campfire, I realized I had seen only two vehicles the entire day—both on the blacktop surface of the Gunflint Trail.

My first encounter with Minnesota's largest mammal, a bull moose, materialized on Finn Lake Road south of Poplar Lake. Finn Lake Road began on the Lima Grade a short distance, maybe two miles, south of the Gunflint Trail near Poplar Lake. From there, it ran due west for approximately six miles and ended near Finn Lake. It, like so many area roads, accessed mature timber south of the Gunflint. From the Finn Lake Road, several spur roads were also used to access timber. Near the south-running Gaskin spur emerged a gigantic bull moose.

There it stood, taking up space crosswise on the narrow

road. Its magnificent, glistening ebony fur overwhelmed the heavy autumn setting. With every exhale from the beast, frost formed on the still morning air. Awestruck by his immenseness I stared at the enormous rack. With the moose's superior size and dominant attitude, it had little to fear, especially from a little chugging black Model A pickup.

It stood maybe 50 yards away. I dared not to shut off the engine. Blowing the oooga horn was not wise. Fear struck me when it laid its ears back and pawed at the ground. I felt vulnerable in the presence of the mammoth creature even though I was inside the cab of the truck.

The standoff ended when I acted submissive and backed the truck away a great distance. Years later, in the same area, I found a massive, time-bleached, rodent-chewed moose shed. I kept it for years and often wondered if it was from the first unforgettable bull moose I had encountered.

Midday, I realized how much I enjoyed simply traveling, negotiating, and exploring the ever-available side roads. This trip was turning out to be an exhilarating search for wilderness pathways. Grouse hunting was secondary. To my surprise, I discovered that several abandoned railroad spurs of the General Logging Company were still negotiable by the Model A. (Several years later "Charlie Boy" Boostrom shared with me that he and his brothers salvaged and sold railroad spikes for scrap iron during World War II.)

Already I had discovered four huge sawdust piles at different locations in this adventure: Greenwood River, Vista Lake, East Bearskin Lake, and Swan Lake. Much later on Friday, near dusk, I came upon a fifth sawdust pile on the South Lake Trail.

This pile, although not high, covered an extensive area on the ridge past Dunn Lake overlooking the international border and South Lake. The Model A actually left ruts in the sawdust as the determined truck crept up and over the now deep-orange, rust-hued remains of white pine.

In 2009, I shared my South Lake sawdust pile truck climb with Bob Johnston, longtime Poplar Lake resident. He definitely recalled seeing the truck ruts when his family fished Dunn Lake.

That evening, on the shore of South Lake, as the last of the migrating loons wailed and I poked at the hot embers of my campfire, I contemplated the enormous number of massive-girth pines it took to create such colossal piles of sawdust.

On Saturday morning it wasn't rain or snow that forced me out of the sleeping bag at dawn; it was sheer, bitter cold, driven across the lake by a Canadian north wind. Had it not been for the north wind, shore ice would have formed around the perimeter of South Lake overnight. In fact, I witnessed ice on many small lakes all day.

"Uh-oh," I said out loud as I jostled over the terrain, making my journey back to the Gunflint Trail early Saturday morning.

The gas tank on the Model A sat under the windshield stretching from the driver's door to the passenger's door. The tank actually formed the dashboard, spanning the same area. How simple and efficient was this! To allow gas to flow to the carburetor, a gas valve was opened near the feet on the passenger side of the cab. Because of the tank's elevated position, no fuel pump was required; gravity did the task.

In the center, mounted to the gas tank halfway between the driver and passenger, were four significant instruments: the key ignition switch, the combination speedometer and odometer, the ammeter gauge, and the gas gauge. A nerve-chilling sensation overcame me when I saw the gas gauge dial intermittently display a stamped black zero (empty) on the revolving brass cylinder.

The gauge was simple. Attached to the brass metered cylinder was a rod with an honest-to-goodness floating cork on the other end. As the gas descended in the tank, so did the cork. Thus the brass cylinder gauge displayed a fraction representing the portion of gas remaining in the tank.

I had seen the bouncing "zero" on previous outings, but never this far from home. Not completely filled with terror of running out because I carried a full five gallons of spare gas, I still had to deal with the issue mentally for the remainder of the day and Sunday.

Since the "zero" was bouncing, I assumed the tank still contained one or two gallons of gas. Hence, when I funneled the spare five gallons of gas into the 10-gallon tank, the gauge indicated nearly three-quarters full. Could I achieve my goal of reaching the end of the Gunflint Trail and Saganaga Lake and still get back to Grand Marais to refuel?

First, I believed I could, as long as I drove to the end of the Trail first and limited the trips on side roads. Second, I would stop to inquire about gas at Gunflint Lodge or any available resort near the Sag landing.

The manifold heat from the manifold engine heater filled the cab with warmth. Unique design allowed air to enter the iron device behind the radiator, flow over the hot iron of the engine, and exit rear of the manifold directly into the passenger side of the cab at foot level.

By the time I reached the magnificent Gunflint Lake overlook, cab heat permeated my extremities. For the first time that day, I was able to grasp the hard-rubber-coated steering wheel with bare hands—no gloves needed. As I turned onto the road to Gunflint Lodge, two white-tailed deer swiftly crossed the gravel road, headed toward the lake. No longer did they carry their thin summer red fur coats. Now they were prepared for the long, brutal winter with a thick, hollow, long, guard-hair coat.

When I got to the lodge and shut off the engine, I didn't get out. I just sat and stared at the Canadian shore. Here I was, by myself, surveying the grand country that my great-great-grandparents had once called home.

It was moments before I realized nobody at the lodge was around, nor were there any boats with outboards on the waterfront.

Finding no gas available at the lodge, soon I was motoring northwest toward Saganaga on the Gunflint Trail. Before long, the blacktop road surface ended. Numerous potholes filled with ice, along with the pit run gravel surface, constituted a unique driving experience. The final miles of the Trail ran between lofty outcroppings of volcanic bedrock, skirted Labrador tea bogs, and culminated at the southern tip of a bay on Saganaga Lake just north of Seagull Lake.

How could such a popular spring and summer fishing destination now be totally deserted? The USFS campground was closed. Both large and small outfitters were closed. Resorts, such as End of the Trail and Chik-Wauk, were uninhabited. In addition, many entrances to private cabins were barricaded. This was not what I had expected. Prospects of finding gasoline were poor.

Why not drive the county road to End of the Trail and Chik-Wauk Resort? So doing, I once again found myself at the end of the road in the Model A. Break time. Stretch time. Time to strategize.

While sitting on the running board having a snack, I listened to the breeze in the multitude of jackpines surrounding the tranquil setting. I noticed bent cattail leaves at oblique angles along the shore, jackpine cones clinging tightly to dead branches in the peak of the tress, and rustling grass and leaves along the hillside with a southern exposure. Then I heard a distant outboard.

What a surprise! Except for an occasional passing vehicle on the blacktop surface, I realized I had not encountered another soul since Wednesday, three days ago. Was I about to encounter a person?

The outboard motor sound gained amplitude. It was approaching. Why?

Momentarily the boat and occupant appeared,. Thin, crackling ice reverberations drifted to me in the noon breeze. Gleefully I sat while the aluminum watercraft and its occupant made their way south in the narrow bay until they finally nudged the gravel shore within 50 feet of the truck.

I sprang to my feet, rushed to the boat, and steadied the bow while a middle-aged man made his way over the seats to the bow and out.

"Thank you, what happened to Don, and by Jesus you got a gem of a truck. I haven't seen a Model A truck in at least 19 years," spoke the wiry man in a well-worn red and black Woolrich jacket.

We never did introduce ourselves, but I learned he had come seven miles by boat from his Canadian island home to get his mail, delivered by Don Brazell from Grand Marais. This trip was probably the last one until the ice became solid and safe to travel on by dogsled. He estimated safe ice travel in five or six weeks.

Of course, the conversation eventually led to his inquiry about my means of transportation. After briefly explaining my Duluth origin and present five-day journey, he became wholeheartedly supportive, and even volunteered to retrieve five gallons from his cache of winter gas so I could get back to Grand Marais. Our bond grew even stronger when he shared he was a graduate of the 1940 Duluth Denfeld class.

The chatter between us ceased when around the pond mailman Don's vehicle was spotted. I couldn't have been more fortunate or had better timing. My gas predicament was explained to Don. Of course, being a mailman, he knew who lived where and where I could obtain spare fuel. Both the fellows looked my transportation over and the stories of Model A escapades lasted extensively.

With Don's advice came a warning. He concurred with my findings that many businesses were shut down for the season, except for possibly one, that being Trail Center on Poplar Lake. Fred and Thelma Liebertz had closed their restaurant much earlier, but hung around for a while to enjoy late autumn days. I did recall seeing a single gas pump off the blacktop when I passed the business yesterday. However, he did warn me that occasionally, for no apparent reason, they would refuse a sale or to sell gas. It was best to get in and out quickly.

Another option for gas were Carl and Alis Brandt, the nice folks at Balsam Grove Resort on Poplar Lake. Certainly, if desperate, they could find enough gas to get me to town. Or finally, Don said, if worse comes to worse, you just hail some vehicle down on the Gunflint for a ride to town with your empty five-gallon can. He explained that vehicles on the road at this time of year were driven by locals, who would help.

That was my first and last encounter with the legendary mailman, Don Brazell.

Encouraged and now restless to roll and make the most of the rest of Saturday, I bid goodbye to the owner of the boat as he loaded boxes of supplies into his watercraft. He leaped out of his boat, wished me luck, and suggested if I ever get back to Sag to look him up. Quickly he turned and checked his mailbox one last time before I pushed him off.

I glanced at the name on his mailbox, turned and entered the cab, hit the foot starter, and got a thumbs up from "Benson" as the Ford pickup came to life and headed down the trail.

For the next 50 years. I always enjoyed my visits with Irv Benson, especially in the winter after my retirement. Irv's close friends, Dave and Carol Seglum, prepared a beautiful memorial service on July 3, 2009 in honor of his life. The service was held at Chippewa Inn on Red Pine Island on the Ontario side of Saganaga Lake, near Irv's home.

My focus that Saturday afternoon wasn't on my fall dream trip, nor was it on the scenery of the upper Gunflint Trail as I dawdled my way to the Rib Lake Trail. Instead, my mind was intrigued and fascinated by a lifestyle without the usual amenities of modern city living. This brief encounter of such a lifestyle on Saganaga Lake late in October smoldered in the recesses of my mind for nearly a dozen years.

After high school, after four years of college and with a doctoral degree nearly completed, the rural lifestyle concept no longer smoldered—it burst into flames. The mental struggle between a relaxed, slow pace of living versus an upscale, stressful career lifestyle reached a compromise. I continued my tenured educator's position in Duluth but spent countless weekends and summers on the Gunflint.

The final evening of my solo autumn excursion to the Gunflint, I camped near a small creek on the Rib Lake Trail. It was a starless night. Through suspicion, senses, or whatever, I surmised a change in the clear, dry, cool weather. Soon it would shift to a more challenging environment. Would it be the first snowfall of autumn, creating a hypothermic rain?

Distant hoots of "Who cooks for you all" from a single barred owl diminished. In the rising smoke above the modest campfire came illusions of Irv Benson on his last motorboat trip of the season for supplies. Without warning, a gust of wind swept through the campfire, spreading the final embers.

No longer did the tongues of the flames illuminate the near bark of the paper birch. No longer did the dusky, satanic shadows dance in the peripheral forest. No longer did the flat glass of the dual headlights on the Model A glimmer and glow in the campfire shades of yellow, orange and red. The final evening of an exhilarating October journey had drawn to a close.

By morning, a dismal mix of sleet and snow descended from the low, dense stratus ceiling. Sleet clung to the evergreen branches until the boughs of green could hold no more. Cascades of swooshes came from all directions as I packed the camping gear in the box of the Model A for the final time. Thankfully, the "Norvegan" boot grease applied to my 8-inch leather boots kept my feet dry in the sloppy footing.

Because of the sleet, breakfast was kept to a minimum. Today my objective was to reach Duluth—home—by late afternoon. For the first time in four days, I thought about my parents and the concerns they might have had for me. We didn't have any way to communicate with each other except through prayers.

Fortunately, this sloppy snow was not slippery for driving. The truck's tires cut through the mushy covering to the surface below as I made my way down the Trail to the single gas pump at Trail Center. There was absolutely no doubt I needed gas.

Boldly I drove up to the pump, paused briefly before getting out, not knowing exactly what to expect, heeding the words of Don. Once I got out of the cab I retrieved the five-gallon spare gas can from under a tarp in the box. Pausing further, I brushed the snow from around the chrome gas cap and looked at my watch, which read 10:30. Behind me I heard a door creak open. It was a jacketed and rubber-booted Fred.

I thought this was a positive sign and politely stated, "I would like to buy 10 gallons of gas," holding up my gas can and pointing to the gas cap of the truck. I didn't recognize his mutterings as he shuffled to the truck. I did hear his brief, complimentary comments about my transportation. "Good condition. Never seen this Model A around here before."

While he was filling the truck, I hastily wrote out a $2 check to Trail Center. Immediately after he rehung the gas pump hose, I handed him the check. I didn't wait for a response (not knowing if he would accept it), lifted the full spare gas can into the box, and courteously said "Thank you" as I entered the cab. In the rear-view mirror, I still vividly recall Fred standing by the pump looking bewildered at both the check from a Duluth institution and the black Model A Ford pickup leaving a set of tracks in the slush to the roadway. Thank you, Fred.

Being young and writing a $2 check, I didn't feel deceitful. A couple of things need to be explained. First, it was 1959, and gasoline, even on the Gunflint Trail, sold for 20 cents a gallon. Hence, 10 gallons cost $2. (As a side note, the Model A pickup averaged 20 miles per gallon so it was possible for me to reach Duluth on my available fuel supply.) Secondly, I never had, nor carried, an excess of cash. Many times I would leave Duluth, gas tank and spare gas can full, with $5-10 cash. Truly I was trusting God and good luck. Finally, were there credit cards in that era? If so, I didn't possess one. There certainly weren't "pay at the pump" stations.

The closer I got to Grand Marais, the less and less slush, sleet and snow there was, until I was driving in rain. Back and forth went the single-speed windshield wiper blade, powered by the Model A's six-volt battery and wiper motor.

The trip home was anticlimactic except for my jubilant parents' reception. Over supper I shared stories and felt a sense of admiration from my father's smiles.

3

Four Hour Traveling Experiences

Football season, deer-hunting season, and Thanksgiving passed. With alacrity the holiday season approached. What a joyous period as relatives across the nation returned to their roots in northern Minnesota.

During this festive time, I bent the ears of many uncles regarding my past summer's solo Model A trips to the Gunflint. Fortunately, I was able to convince my relatives from Kansas to book their first of many summer vacations at Chik-Wauk Resort on Saganaga Lake. Actually, them being avid fishermen, it was a no-brainer once the new owners, Ralph and Bea Griffis of Chik-Wauk Lodge, sent them a colorful, fish-filled brochure. Ralph, a native Texan, and my uncle Duane, who worked in the oil fields of the South, developed a lasting friendship. Imagine the anticipation I experienced for the six months prior to arriving at Chik-Wauk.

Brown log-sided cabins, nightly bear visits, feeding half-dead bait minnows to Ralph's pet northerns, and evening dinners in the stone dining hall are all part of the glorious experience and hospitality we experienced at Chik-Wauk. Besides the outstanding walleye fishing, I was able to reunite with Irv.

One evening, after Irv had guided fishermen for End of the Trail Lodge, he stopped at the request of Ralph to see an old friend. I had discussed with Ralph my accidental meeting

Sister Jan and friend on the dock at Chik-Wauk Resort.

with Irv the previous fall and had no idea Irv was invited for dinner with my relatives. On his way into the dining hall, Irv's keen eye spotted the Model A at Cabin 1. When he entered the hall, he glanced over the crowd until his eyes identified the truck's younger owner, whereupon he came over and surprised me with a hardy handshake. Of course, Bea immediately set a place for him at our table.

Irv was known for his ability to eat, I later learned, but during the course of this meal he couldn't stop yakking about this kid from Duluth, by himself, and his Ford Model A pickup at Sag just before freeze-up last fall. Later that week, I was able to once again see Irv, this time at his Pine Island Resort on the Ontario side of Saganaga Lake. There I was introduced to his wife, Tempest Powell Benson. Over the years, I learned about the historic events of the area and developed a deep admiration for the Powell family.

Many times that summer, I made fishing trips to the Gunflint in the black pickup. Because I had a part-time job commitment, I often left Duluth around 10 p.m. The trips to Saganaga were especially challenging. For sure, after 11 p.m. gas stations were closed, but gas wasn't the biggest headache—staying awake was. If I had shared this concern with my parents, I might have lost their strong support.

The greatest distance was to Chik-Wauk. However, there I could refuel at Ralph's Shell pump. The same was true at Clearwater Lodge; gas was available in the summer. To avoid falling asleep, I cultivated a taste for sucking on hard candy. Lemon drops were my favorite, but hot cinnamon kept me alert the best.

Even the spiciest cinnamon had its downfall during one steady rain. For some reason, the combination of the warmth of the simple heater, the monotonous drone of the engine, the hypnotizing effect of the one single-speed windshield wiper, and the weak headlights peering into the continuous darkness was an accident waiting to happen.

Traveling on the North Shore of Lake Superior on Highway 61 was much different in those days. There was virtually no roadside habitation. Milepost markers didn't exist, nor did multiple highly reflective signs. Billboard advertising and even state park signs were few and far between. There was very little oncoming traffic. Developments didn't exist. From Duluth to Pigeon River, only a handful of stoplights existed, counting the in-town flashing lights. Thus, there was a lack of stimulus, even on a moonless night. True, there was always the possibility of hitting wildlife, but not at the snail's pace I traveled.

As a result, in addition to spiced hard candy, I acquired a variety of techniques to keep the Model A on the road. Stopping and getting out for fresh air was somewhat helpful. However, drowsiness quickly returned, and besides, I lost time with each stop. Traveling with one or both windows down was effective. Besides, it involved motion, steering concentration, and plenty of cool, fresh air off Lake Superior.

Taking my foot off the gas pedal and using the hand throttle was partially effective, but least desirable should an animal cross the road or I encounter curves in the road. Probably most effective in maintaining alertness was to keep a moist washcloth on the seat in a dishpan and wipe my face when I recognized drowsiness.

That was the key: to recognize drowsiness. On one swarthy night, I didn't recognize drowsiness. My head dropped, and the jerk caused a heads-up, eyes-open reflex reaction. Thankfully, I was on my half of the pavement. Startled but still torpid I continued. Shortly I felt my eyes begin to close. The road narrowed, the view went out of focus, and the headlights went dim. For moments I heard the drone of the engine, but saw nothing.

Mental attempts were made to steer the pickup down the

presumed center of the pavement without vision. Was I asleep? Surely, or I would have decelerated. What next? No rumble strips, very little shoulder, then what?

Mentally, subconsciously, willing myself to an elevated level of alertness, slowly my vision returned. A lifelong image imprinted on my memory of traveling millimeters from a guardrail along the extreme edge of the blacktop—going in the wrong direction in the other lane.

Silent expressions of prayer were given daily for a week for the blessing of my safety.

Other jaunts in the spirited, diminutive Model A required little effort to stay awake. No, I didn't use a caffeinated beverage. Instead, Mother Nature provided three distinguished overhead shows: lightning, northern lights, and a full moon.

As a youngster I was warned of the dangers of lightning. "Get off the lake before the thunderstorm reaches you" is good advice. "Don't get under tall trees with the threat of lightning" is another valid truth, just as is "Don't camp under tall trees." Yet it is safe to ride in a vehicle during a heavy electrical storm, which I did on occasion along Lake Superior en route to the Gunflint in the Model A. During such storms, I witnessed a plethora of lightning flashes, which for moments lit up the entire landscape.

The most spectacular flashes occurred over Lake Superior. Periodically in the darkness, ore carrier lights could be seen on the big lake, when suddenly a wicked bolt of lightning flashed in the vicinity, allowing me to see the carrier's outline. Such flashes would keep me awake and pondering, "Why aren't the iron-hulled ore carriers in peril on Lake Superior?"

Have you ever seen the moon rise over Lake Superior? The show can last for hours. My favorite full moons over Lake Superior occurred in the fall. The moon glitters on the waters of Lake Superior best in the cool air. At times, a long silver streak forms a direct path between you and the glowing orb in the dark sky. Other times, spiral spruce tops come between you and the moon, creating bewitching scenes.

Because Highway 61 between Duluth and Grand Marais run in a northeasterly direction, the brilliant moon provided ample stimulus to keep me from drowsiness. At times, the higher the moon rose, the better the show because of the assortment and shape of clouds passing in front of the moon. Only the howl of the gray wolf could surpass the primordial sensation in me created by fast-traveling, wafer-thin clouds in front of a full moon on a cold evening when I was on my way up to the Gunflint in the Ford pickup.

Other chilly evenings while covering the path to the Gunflint I was entertained by the aurora borealis. Never did I witness the stupendous electromagnetic drama that one can experience in the extreme far north of Canada or Alaska. However, three observations were extraordinary. Many people witness pale or light green aurora borealis. One clear autumn evening, obviously dark and moonless, I watched for almost an hour as pale green probes quickly rose from the northern landscape and just as rapidly retreated back to the horizon. These dancing probes marched from the east to the west and then appeared again in the east. Sometimes a few soft, mellow green spires rose directly overhead, while shorter spires danced up and down like an electronic screen on a heart monitor.

On another occasion, I sat mystified in the Model A at the Gunflint Lake overlook. Above the Canadian landscape, pulsating in size, flattened against the ionosphere, loomed a feathery pastel-yellow figure eight.

It didn't move. Instead, it remained in a constant position, pulsating in strength or amplitude like a distant crystal radio signal. So perfect a figure eight was it, and so transfixed on it was I, that it wasn't until I was about step on the floor starter and proceed to Saganaga Lake that I recognized on the flat mirror surface of Magnetic Lake a reflection of the overhead figure eight.

The reflection was much weaker and then nonexistent when the heavenly figure eight's radiance diminished. But when the heavenly eight intensified so did the aquatic eight. Who knows how long I observed the phenomenon? Fifteen minutes? Thirty minutes? It was still visible when I determined it was time to get rolling.

No other vehicle appeared on the blacktopped Gunflint Trail as I witnessed this midnight spectacle. I wonder if any other humans observed the phenomenon of the heavenly eight from the cabins or resorts on the south shore of Gunflint Lake.

The third borealis phenomenon that kept me alert while making the nocturnal sojourn to the Gunflint I called the "red curtain."

On rural roads after dusk, away from the city lights, the wonders of nature and space stimulate one's visual acuity. Who hasn't pondered the immensity of the universe, the composition of the Milky Way, the plethora of constellations, or even the craters of the moon? But just suppose, while traveling on a clear, cloudless night on desolate stretches of the Gunflint Trail, all heavenly bodies vanish as a subtle red curtain materializes between you and the thousand points of light in space.

At first the red curtain isn't obvious as the road twists and turns and the Model A passes in the shadows of majestic white pines and other species that cloak the Trail's shoulders. The rational mentality would say it's a layer of clouds. But forced by curiosity to stop, shut off the engine, and turn out the headlights, I realize that nearly all of the sky is covered in a soft, dark-red hue. Strange!

Forest fire? No! With absolutely no perceivable change overhead after minutes of observation, overcome with the chill of midnight air, I resumed my journey. The red curtain was almost forgotten as I made my way to my West Bearskin cabin.

However, standing on the porch looking due north on the last trip of the night into the cabin, the red curtain rose above the mighty pines on the north shore of West Bearskin Lake. I looked at my watch: 1:30 a.m.

The soft red curtain continued to rise higher and higher, obliterating stars, until once again all I could see of the sky was red. Amazing.

4

The Rush To Rose

Prior to 1965, when we built a cabin on state-leased land on West Bearskin Lake, Dad and I would spend Memorial Day weekend camping and fishing on Rose Lake.

The foray to the border lake would commence the Friday before Memorial Day at approximately four in the afternoon. That was the earliest Dad could get home from work. As always, the Model A was packed with gear the night before. Dad let me drive now, maybe because were going to "my country."

I always pushed the little truck to its maximum speed, which meant near 50 mph. It was a race against time and darkness. Our goal was to reach the first campsite west of the Stairway Portage on Rose Lake before darkness. Because we ate sandwiches in the truck, carried extra gas, and were effi-

Last minute adjustments.

128

ciently packed, we often had our tent up before having to light the kerosene lantern.

Having daylight until nearly 10 p.m. was a big help. On many clear evenings, we commented on the band of glowing light on the northern horizon, referring to the "land of the midnight sun."

The shortest land-and-water route to the Stairway Portage was from the West Bearskin Lake access off Hungry Jack Road. Often when we arrived at the access on a Friday, we had the small parking lot to ourselves.

To further facilitate crossing West Bearskin and Duncan Lake, we used an outboard motor attached to a side mount on the canoe. The archaic outboard with its exposed flywheel—which required a rope to start—steadily pushed the canoe. Oh, how good it felt to have the tent up and sleeping bags unrolled. The first evening, the roar of the waterfall was a constant noise, but by the following day we would grow accustomed to the sound of the water cascading off the ledge rock near Duncan Lake and plummeting 138 feet to the rocky shore of Rose Lake.

In those early years, prior to the creation of the Boundary Waters Canoe Area Wilderness (BWCAW), we had the whole border lake to ourselves for the entire extended weekend. Many hours were spent in the canoe fishing the waters for the elusive lake trout. The tiny Lauson outboard held less than one quart of gas, yet we could troll for an entire day without refueling.

Sometimes we would land a northern on the strip-on baits. Other times it would be a lake trout. Occasionally we would catch a beautiful whitefish.

Any fish we couldn't eat was put on ice, which we found deep in the recesses of the large rock wall between the two lakes. On this weekend, ice was always present on the north face out of the direct rays of the sun.

Besides the lack of campers, other differences in this area existed compared to 50 years later. Many campsites had picnic tables provided by the U.S. Forest Service. Both the beginning and end of portages had earthen or log cribs for easy access into and out of a canoe. The Civilian Conservation Corps (CCC) constructed these cribs during the 1930s.

Many portages were narrow, but laid smooth with dirt. The dirt was held in place by log "shoulders" to prevent washouts or erosion. In addition, muddy or bog stretches of the portage were elevated and planked with half logs. Many long portages had canoe rests. On portages with a steep gradient, real log staircases were built primarily of native white cedar for travelers. On many occasions over the log Stairway Portage, I counted 120 steps.

Wooden routered signs identified many landmarks, lakes and points of interest—not just along the Gunflint Trail road, but also in the heart of the forest. Deer and moose were abundant. It was a rare trip when we didn't spot deer on the shoreline of a lake. More than once, we found a magnificent moosehorn shed on a portage on our Memorial weekend trip. Lastly, big northerns were prevalent in large number in numerous lakes, with smallmouth bass being an inferior minority species.

On Memorial Day itself, a Monday, fishing was not a pri-

Camping on the Gunflint Trail.

ority—breaking camp was. With our trip near completion, our food pack was lighter, as was the outboard gas can. Still, climbing the 120 steps on the Stairway Portage was a daunting task.

Fully loaded down with packs and miscellaneous gear while shouldering the canoe, I carefully selected each foot placement on the slippery, worn log steps. Not until I reached the last step did I hear the constant roar of the waterfall. With weary, rubbery legs, a pounding heart, and heaving lungs gasping for oxygen, I continued on the short, level stretch of remaining portage to the protected cove on Duncan Lake.

We had traversed the Stairway Portage climb in a single trip. At the cove under the overhanging cedar branches we had moments to rest. Dark, weathered logs under cedar trees restricted the outflow of water from Duncan Lake before it tumbled over and through strewn boulders to the edge of the waterfall.

Even though the water in the cove appeared on the surface to be calm, blades of submerged grass pointed and waved in the direction of the outlet. Small pieces of organic matter

At the base of the Stairway Portage, Bob is ready to shove off on Rose Lake.

tumbled along the bottom until it, too, was swiftly drawn between the logs and gone—to Rose Lake, Arrow Lake or Lake Superior, or trapped in a crevice along the portage.

As we loaded the canoe for the journey across Duncan, its bow was also caught in the unpretentious current and drawn down to the outlet. It might have taken ages, but without a doubt, the water that passed beneath the canoe in that tranquil cove would someday reach the Atlantic Ocean via the Saint Lawrence Seaway.

Before the final push-off, my mind flashed back to a similar emotional perspective I had had at Silver Falls two years before.

Silver Falls is the outlet of Saganagons Lake. Two years

previous, I sat and rested at Silver Falls after completing the portage from Saganagons Lake. In the fine mist that shrouded the fragrant white cedar, I pondered the final destination of this water. The water of Silver Falls would eventually, I determined, end up in Hudson Bay. Both of these aquatic revelations could be read and determined by examining an atlas. However, the concept really derives meaning when your senses embrace the magnificence of a waterfall. Truly, water is a wondrous "common" thing on planet Earth.

Little did I know, as I started the Model A at the Hungry Jack-West Bearskin parking lot, that this would be my last Memorial Day Rose Lake camping excursion. I had a dream to own Gunflint property. How could such a dream be realized while I was in college, with few assets—not much money, no real estate knowledge, no established Gunflint connections, not even a steady job? On the flip side, I had determination, enthusiasm, youth, small cash savings, the support of my skilled father, grandfathers and uncle, and, of course, the beloved Model A truck.

5

Leased Lot

Throughout the summer I pondered the dream. The allure of living on a Canadian island in Saganaga ala Irv Benson was powerful, but just not practical for year-round access given my meager means. I did check on individual pieces of property in the upper Gunflint, but again either found the drawbacks or financing a hindrance.

Late in August, I found a solution to my dream in a Sunday news article in the Duluth Herald. The article listed a few parcels of land that the Minnesota DNR would lease in northeastern Minnesota.

There were very few restrictions on the 99-year lease. The fee was affordable, and, best of all, no cash outlay or attorney fees were required. I scrambled to the Duluth DNR land office for West Bearskin Lake details in Cook County. Next, with a copy of the plat map, Dad and I scrambled up to the Gunflint to look over the land parcels.

Several lots, years ago, had been utilized for YMCA Camp Menogyn on the north shore directly across from the available 75-foot wide new lease parcels. Wow! What a vertical drop from the south side of the lot down to the lakeshore. My dad described it as a "Stairway Portage lot." Only one other cabin existed on the state land, meaning it also offered privacy.

All lots and property corners were clearly identified with wooden posts with engraved numerals. Of the dozen or more lots available, one lot had a somewhat level area halfway up the incline. There was no road access to any of the lease parcels. Fortunately, a co-op power line ran along the back or top (south side) of the lots.

I later learned that 10 years earlier, in 1955, electrical energy was brought into Clearwater Lake and Clearwater Lodge. It was along the access to the electrical line that I grubbed a traversable trail for the Model A to the back of my leased lot from the Clearwater Road.

With all the paperwork done, I signed a lease with the state, and for a 25-dollar fee I had fulfilled a dream.

Hunting trips to the ditchbanks north of Duluth were now a thing of the past. All fall forays were to the wilds of the Gunflint Trail.

On each trip north, the Model A carried as many used 8- or 12-inch cement blocks in the box as Dad would allow. Eventually I had transported enough cement blocks to lay or stack on the perimeter of the ground around an 18 foot by 28 foot cabin. Why would we haul cement blocks in a tiny pickup from Duluth to West Bearskin Lake on the Gunflint? Simple: The cement blocks were free, I was going up the Trail to hunt, and I knew of no Grand Marais source.

Late that October, with leaves on the ground, I found myself on the end of a hand shovel, grubbing roots and rocks, laying and leveling, and squaring cement blocks.

That fall, arrangements were made and temporary electrical service was installed at the cabin. For no charge, Arrowhead Electric Cooperative erected a utility pole, installed a meter, and hooked up a temporary construction outlet loop. Amazing! All this work was done within two weeks of my telephone request. Also astonishing was the fact that with the yearly fee I received 400 free kilowatts of electricity.

Over many of my three-day breaks from the University of Minnesota-Duluth, I would head to the Gunflint. A college schedule was different than a high school schedule. My class schedule varied from quarter to quarter. Often during a particular quarter of school I had four days of class and a three-day break, plus the usual designated holidays. I took full advantage of those breaks. The season didn't matter.

I constructed a primarily one-person plywood topper for the Model A. The purpose of the topper was to provide shelter from the winter elements on the Gunflint. The topper was essentially a pine box, six feet long, 36 inches high and 42 inches wide, with a hinged plywood rear door that slid into the pickup box when the tailgate was chained horizontal to the box floor.

The pine box was nearly airtight, which provided shelter from the arctic night winds. A flashlight was the only source of light unless the hinged door was open. For insulation from the severe cold, the pine box was lined with layers of carpeting and rugs and then stuffed with old quilts and bedding. I slept in a sleeping bag clothed in down underwear, wool socks, and stocking cap. Only once can I say I shivered extensively overnight.

Probably I "camped out" in the Model A a total of 10 or 12 times that winter. Because Clearwater Road was plowed during the winter, I was able to park at the east end of West Bearskin Lake or on a road near Clearwater Lodge. The county snowplow widened the Bearskin access, but it was out in the

Gunflint Trail Pioneers Petra and Charlie Boostrom.

open and exposed to the bitter winds off the lake in January and February.

I much preferred the sheltered areas near the lodge. From there I had snowshoe access to Clearwater, Daniels, Rose, and other trout lakes once the lake trout season opened.

There were never more than one or possibly two vehicles on the Clearwater Road during my winter visits. I later learned that two parties resided year-round on the road in that era, the Boostroms and Billy Needham. Midwinter, after the coldest night I had endured, I was jumping around in the frost-filled morning air to increase my blood circulation when a male voice startled me.

"Are you all right? Do you need a warm-up?"

The snow crunched and squeaked with every step he took as he approached. He continued, "Ya, we've seen your Model

A here a number of times and thought you must stay in it. This morning it was -48 degrees. No telling how cold it got during the night. You're nuts for staying out in temperatures like that. We don't like to mess with strangers, but you could die!"

It sounded like I being scolded by this tall, lank, middle-age, wool-Mackinaw- and Malone-bib-clad local. Regardless, I couldn't resist his invitation to warm up at his place.

After a brisk walk down what is now named Petra Lane, we entered a beautiful split-face stone house. Instantly my pale white cheeks flushed as my face absorbed the luxurious warmth from the wood stove. Before long, I was sitting at the kitchen table with hot coffee and pancakes. This was my first meeting with the Gunflint trailblazer, Charlie Boostrom, and his wife, Petra.

Apparently my winter visits in the Model A had created much discussion over the course of the winter. It was the elder Boostroms who, out of concern for my survival, sent their youngest son, Glen, to check on me that morning. It was the beginning of a long friendship lasting several generations. In the years to come, especially during the winter, Glen counseled me on numerous Gunflint issues.

"Goodness, it was up to minus 40," proclaimed Petra. "A real pleasant day." If I hadn't been before, I was now a black coffee drinker.

I took more away from that morning than a warm body, though. I made connections in Cook County through their friendship, which proved to be useful in future times of need. Conversely, I earned their respect and admiration for my hardy solo adventures.

When Glen learned I wanted to build a cabin, he told me about Hedstrom's Lumber Mill. He advised me not to haul lumber from Duluth in the Model A, as Hedstrom's would deliver. He said they had all building materials and excellent quality, locally milled and kiln-dried lumber. I was elated.

Armed with a Grand Marais lumber source, I spent the evening hours drawing plans for the small cabin on West Bearskin. When spring break arrived, instead of heading for the southern beaches, I pointed the Model A in the direction of Grand Marais.

Upon Glen's recommendation, I asked for Herb Hedstrom to assist me with my order and look over my drawings. At Hedstrom's wholesale yard on Highway 61, shortly after I got in the front door, a clerk yelled, "Hey, Herb, come look at the nice Model A pickup this fellow has."

The little black Model A once again opened doors and lines of communication in a way I never could have. Herb had ample carpentry experience. He shared Model A experiences and found my plans to be excellent and easy to work from. What service I got!

Once the snow melted, Hedstrom's delivered building materials on Fridays for my weekend carpentry crew. The crew consisted of my dad, at least one grandfather, frequently my uncle Kenny, and me. Every Friday, an accurate delivery was made by Hedstrom's until July 4th, when the cabin basics were completed.

Somebody had to do it, it was my cabin, and I was the youngest, so I hauled the lumber down the hill to the other men. We cut a trail to the cabin site for the Model A. We used the trail primarily for hauling roofing materials in the truck, but I hauled lumber, plywood and timbers by hand since that material was lengthy and wouldn't stay in place even on the canoe rack.

We planned the best we could for plumbing, electrical and other supplies. However, once I had to make a Saturday trip to town in the Model A for a single copper fitting.

It was a must, to finish the plumbing, but what a waste of time. One copper sweat-on fitting – ¾" to ½" reducer—then $0.19 at Midway Hardware. No wonder in the bush everything, every scrap, gets saved. Still, cabin owners try to exist under the premise that if they haul a truck or car trunk full of stuff to the cabin every time they go, then after 30 years they've got to have what they need to do the necessary job or repair.

Wrong! Murphy's Law...

Needless to say, the skills I learned while erecting the West Bearskin cabin have served me well. Cement and cement block laying, carpentry, plumbing, water systems, paint and staining, metal working, roofing, heating, and electrical applications, to name just a few. I also learned use of tools, safety considerations, and some common sense.

One particular instance of common sense—or, rather, lack of it—sticks out in my memory. Dad didn't like the way I tossed unwanted materials from the roof, ladder or scaffolding, and he let me know it. I could see his point. I thought I was tossing things clear of harm's way.

Near the very end of the project, the only major thing left to do was to disconnect the constructed electrical loop and secure the 100 amp entrance electrical service wires to the high-voltage wires atop the power pole by the transformer. This would provide the electricity inside to all the waiting circuits.

My dad encouraged me to climb the pole and make the connections. He proclaimed it to be a safe task as long as I only made contact with one "line" at a time. I was scared, but, after all that Dad and the other men had done for me, I didn't want to show my fear or disappoint them. So up the pole I went on borrowed pole climbers.

With tremendous apprehension I separated the three lines with a stout wood maul handle. Next, I disconnected each construction loop wire from the high-voltage leads. Finally, I attached the 100 amp cabin service lines to the high-voltage lines one at a time with the proper connectors. As a final measure, I rechecked the torque on all connectors with the crescent wrench. While I was still at the top of the pole, Dad flipped the main breaker and light beamed brightly around the cabin. Success!

Dad returned to the pole to watch me climb down. My legs were beginning to feel weak. Since I didn't have a tool belt (wrenches were stuffed in jeans pockets and hindered fluid movement), I asked if I could drop the big, clumsy wrench. The answer was, "Sure." So not wanting to toss the wrench and irritate dad, what did I do? I simply held it out close to the power pole and let it go.

CLINK! The wrench hit the glass meter case and cracked it. Sometimes you try to please, but… Murphy's Law. Fortunately, we didn't lose power, nor was the meter mechanism compromised.

6
Winter Cabin Chores

Fishing wasn't a priority that summer. Gradually summer led to fall. That fall, while still enrolled at UMD, textbooks accompanied my forays to the Gunflint. Rainy Saturdays were no longer a disappointment as I sat in comfort inside the cabin, studying.

When outdoors, and especially when grouse hunting, I always carried a new acquisition: a 110 McCulloch chainsaw. Whenever a downed dead tree blocked a logging road while grouse hunting, I cut the tree to firewood length. One average tree cut up was all the pickup box could hold. By the end of October, I had a great pile of split firewood for the hungry Franklin stove for the upcoming winter.

There are those who love the challenges of living in a cold climate for part of a year. I am one of them. Once a blanket of snow covers the ground and seals the ponds and lakes, true winter has arrived. Animal tracks, large and small, beg to be identified. Numerous birds remain active under the harsh conditions.

Even the plants have adaptations for winter. Many plants have set buds in place at the tips of the new growth; these buds sit in place all winter, waiting for the spring sun to return. Even though fish are cold-blooded they adjust to a lower lake water temperature, as hardy ice fishermen know.

My parents and relatives embraced the winter season. Thus, they never questioned why, after a robust Thanksgiving dinner, I would excuse myself and head for the Gunflint in the Model A. Very often I would arrive at West Bearskin late in the evening. During the snow season, the Model A was left parked at the West Bearskin landing. From there, I tobogganed supplies three blocks to the cabin.

The first chore was to light a fire in the Franklin wood stove to warm up the cabin. This heating process took several hours. By the next morning the cabin was comfortable (except for the floor). Wood burned quickly in the Franklin and had to be refueled several times an hour. Still, in the wild spirit of the Gunflint, I preferred the wood stove over the propane or electric space heaters.

While the cabin was warming up that first night, I did other chores. In the winter, I never hauled water from home in Duluth to the cabin. Why? Because even a five-gallon jug of water would freeze solid if hauled in the pickup box exposed to the boreal temperatures. There wasn't room in the cab of the Model A once the groceries and winter garments were on the passenger side. The groceries were protected from the freezing drafts by the surplus garments. There never was adequate heat in the cab in the depths of winter.

So water for consumption, cooking and washing came from the lake. Regardless of the winter conditions—bitter cold, starry nights, heavy snowfall, or high winds—it was a task to get water. On the porch I always left the critical items used to get water: an ice chisel, saucepan, and five-gallon pails. To chop through the ice with a sharp ice chisel required varying degrees of effort, depending upon the thickness of the ice. Usually by Christmas the ice had grown to a foot thick, by

February two feet, and by March three feet. The thicker the ice, the more work it took. I would get so exhausted chopping that if heavy slush were present above the ice level, I'd scoop the slush as a water supply instead.

Other nights' conditions dictated I put my back to the wind, flip the parka hood up, and simultaneously chop and remove the ice chips until water gurgled into the chiseled reservoir. At times while resting, it was possible to hear snow crystals rolling across the frozen surface.

When the ice was thickest and there was no wind, I would begin to get warm chopping a water hole. "Whew, this parka is coming off." Even though getting a water supply was tedious and challenging, it was extremely satisfying to obtain one of the necessary rudiments of life.

Soon, hand ice augers were perfected and preferred by ice fishermen over spuds (a common term for ice chisels). It wasn't long before power ice augers could be heard on popular fishing lakes. I always preferred the simplicity of the chisel to the power augers. No gas to mix and carry, no recoil starters to freeze, and no noise.

Has anyone heard of an electric ice auger? Leave it to my dad to design one. He mounted a Model A electric starter motor on a shaft of an ice auger. The starter motor electric lead wires were directly attached to the positive and negative posts of the Model A truck's 6-volt battery. A flip of an inline switch was all that it took for the auger to spin and quickly cut a hole. With the Model A engine running, you never had to worry about discharging the battery. Of course, the truck had to be on the ice where you wanted to fish.

Richard and Kenny Olson hard at work on the cabin..

In the beam of the flashlight, pristine, crystal-clear water gushed to the top of the ice hole. After a few well-placed chops of the chisel, the aperture of the hole was wide enough for the saucepan. The ice chips were scooped aside and the five-gallon pail filled to near the top.

Now the real struggle began. With leather mittens (called choppers) on, flashlight in one hand and the pail in the other, I slogged through snow up the steep incline to the cabin. By the time I reached the porch, I probably had four gallons of water remaining in the pail.

With a pounding heart from ice chopping and carrying water uphill, it was time for a rest before returning to the lake for more water. During the break, I filled a teakettle with water and put it on the woodstove.

The teakettle supplied hot water for many uses throughout my stay. The ever-hungry woodstove demanded more chunks

The Olson family at the cabin. Seated in front, Robert Findlay and Alfred Olson. Standing, left to right, are Bob, Richard, Jan and Roberta Olson, Helen Findlay and Helen Olson.

of stored sunlight. Break time was over and a normal heartbeat resumed. The last water pail had to be filled and carried uphill. This was less demanding since the water hole was open and the snowy trail somewhat tromped down.

Few people realize how hard it is to walk through deep snow. Snowshoes could not be used because of the steep incline to the cabin. When the water chore was finally accomplished, I consumed a chilly glass of lake water. How refreshing! No one in those days ever gave a thought to giardia or pollution. We just drank the water straight from the lake. No one ever got sick.

By now, the next chore was usually to shovel a path to the woodshed and the outhouse. It seemed like hauling firewood was a never-ending task. The most important armload was the last one just before you left for home. This armload was the supply you would use to light the urgently needed fire in the

Franklin stove on the next trip.

After a couple of hours, I was settled in for the night at the cabin. People who own cabins must enjoy working. You work to keep the cabin in shape. You work to put up wood for the winter. You work to carry water. I wonder, are people who own cabins healthy as a result?

7

Winter Challenges

In December, a coldness falls upon the land. In January, numb extremities are a part of Fridays in the truck. In February, a survival blanket drapes my left shoulder and legs. Emergency clothing and candy bars must be carried all winter. In March, the days lengthen. Melting compacted snow increases the chance of stretches of ice patches at nightfall.

There is a no margin for travel errors in winter in the sparsely populated Arrowhead region of Minnesota, especially after sunset. If a couple of streetlights weren't on, one would think Grand Marais was closed for the season.

Maybe it was 9:30 p.m.; maybe it was 10:15 p.m. when I fueled up at the Holiday gas station. I was the only customer. Often I wouldn't see another vehicle on the streets of Grand Marais, or, for that matter, on the entire trip up the Gunflint Trail. Subzero winter temperatures kept Cook County residents wisely indoors.

Only if the temperature dropped to minus 40 did my parents object to me going to the cabin. They knew of the hazards of winter travel on desolate roads in a vehicle with inadequate heat, including the possibility of a collision with a moose or deer and the general risks inherent to extreme weather.

If in winter a vehicle has a malfunction or a road accident happens, is the driver prepared for the worst? The tightening of exposed cheeks. Numb toes, then entire feet. Hypothermia. Be prepared! Every Boy Scout knows the motto. and that is exactly how I met the challenges of winter travel to the Gunflint Trail.

The lack of an adequate heater in the Model A presented hurdles to comfortable winter travel. Imagine having to insulate groceries so they don't freeze in the truck's tiny cab. An oversize emergency parka, which I could use if needed, was draped over the cardboard grocery box. The box was on the passenger seat directly in front of what heat came from the engine's manifold heater.

Bitter drafts of exterior air negated the heat. These drafts came through the openings around the floor pedals, clutch, brake, starter, and emergency brake lever. Even the floor-boards—which were literally boards—only had a thin rubber mat to seal the floor drafts. Not much help! The weather seals around the doors and crank-up windows were virtually non-existent.

To avoid coming into direct contact with the drafts, I draped an emergency oversize heavy-duty wool blanket over my left shoulder, lap and legs.

With no other safe ways to heat the cab, to bundle up was a necessity. Let's start at the top. Whether it was a stocking hat or wool Kromer cap, my ears had to be covered. On my chest I usually wore a wool red-and-black plaid shirt over a flannel shirt.

Over the two layers, I would wear a winter parka, complete with hood. Numerous times I had to use the hood on the Gunflint Trail once I got to Hedstrom's mill. Often the warming influence of Lake Superior elevated Grand Marais' temperature. Sometimes the temperature difference between

Grand Marais and Hedstrom's mill was 15 degrees. Imagine on a January night going from minus 15 to minus 30 degrees! At 30 below on the Gunflint Trail I had to use the parka hood to stay warm.

To protect my hands from the hard-rubber-coated metal steering wheel, I wore choppers. Thankfully, my grandmother knit me a pair of wool mitten liners for choppers each year as a Christmas present. These mittens were always greatly appreciated. (I can't help inserting that Grandpa always gave me the leather choppers at Christmas also. I venture to say the grandparents knew the value of these fine gifts.)

Many people today would consider choppers too clumsy for driving. Modern vehicles have many dials and instruments to adjust: radios, CD players, cruise control, wipers, and a plethora of ventilation settings. And, of course, modern vehicles have marvelous heaters.

Layers, layers, layers. You have to keep your legs warm to have warm feet. So I layered clothing on my legs, too: long underwear, light wool pants, and heavyweight wool pants. On some occasions, laces were tied around the cuff end of my pant legs to prevent either cold drafts around the ankles or snow once I got to the cabin. Cotton blue jeans were never adequate or appropriate for winter service.

The snowmobile suit had not been designed yet. There were coveralls, but they were constructed from cotton and inadequate because they didn't repel moisture. Wool was king for warmth and the ability to insulate if wet.

Traveling in winter, my feet often were so cold they became numb. Footwear, to say the least, was primitive. I had watched my grandfather put as many as three pairs of heavy wool socks over his feet before slipping on rubber overshoes. This was his standard practice as he performed his railroad duties outdoors in negative temperatures. Others who performed winter tasks outdoor wore "bunny boots" purchased at a surplus store. It would be another 10 years before insulated pacs, commonly referred to as Sorels, would be the standard for those who worked in the winter elements.

The men who worked in the mines in northern Minnesota were outfitted with special winter leather boots that provided warmth and flexibility to operate machinery. These were the best winter footwear available at the time.

On a Saturday morning in December prior to Christmas, Dad purchased such a pair of boots for me at the Montgomery Wards store in downtown Duluth. What made these 8-inch boots the best was that they had two layers of leather instead of one. They came with a thick, removable wool inner sole. Basically, these boots were purchased one size larger than needed to accommodate wearing a second pair of wool socks. These boots were expensive—$59—but Dad was proud to buy me the best.

I was so proud of those boots I wore them outdoors the remainder of the weekend. Wow! What a difference from single-leather summer-style boots. Those boots provided warmth for my feet like choppers do for the hands. They were light and flexible enough to operate the four floor pedals.

To provide some additional insulation for my feet, I cut a piece of carpeting for the floor on the driver's side, which prevented cold air seepage through the floorboards. However, more than once, due to the cold, I chose to stop on the Gunflint Trail, get out of the cab (never shutting the engine off during the winter), and walk briskly in circles to help the circulation in my feet in the lowest of nighttime temperatures.

Needless to say, traveling in the Model A during winter was a challenge. Under the right humidity and temperature conditions, for instance, frost would form on the inside of the windshield while I was driving.

I used two methods in an attempt to keep a clear view. Rolling down a side door window was not an option due to heat-sapping cold air. So I had to bare a hand and directly place my palm on the glass. Yes, the frost would melt. However, if I moved my palm to another spot, the open transparent spot would quickly freeze with a translucent ice coating.

Again, not a safe way to navigate icy roads. And, of course, my hand became as cold as the icy windshield.

The alternative was to attempt to clear the inside of the windshield of frost by using an ice scraper while negotiating the curves, ice patches, and occasional snow ruts on the road. When I used the ice scraper method, a larger area could be cleared away quickly. However, this method had hazardous drawbacks, too. First I had to locate the ice scraper in the darkness of the cab. Then, using peripheral vision, I had to scrape the windshield while still keeping the truck on the road.

So why not just stop the truck, scrape the frost, and resume driving? Because the scraping method had a drawback. Very quickly after the windshield was initially scraped, another thin layer of frost would develop, and I would have to re-scrape and re-scrape. It was just quicker and easier to scrape on the go.

Obviously, the Model A did not have the windshield defrosters that vehicles possess today. Oh, how we under-appreciate good heaters and defrosters. They make travel in winter safer and more pleasurable.

Starting a 21st-century vehicle in minus 40-degree temperatures is much easier than starting a Model A from the previous century. Today's vehicles come with block and engine heaters, battery heaters, synthetic engine oil, and other doodads that enhance starting. Often, all you have to do is plug in the vehicle and your worries of whether the vehicle will start diminish.

This was not the case when I parked the Model A on winter trips to the Gunflint Trail. Electricity was not available where I parked, nor did the Model A have any electric gizmos to aid starting. But I learned tricks from the northlanders. These were very important because, unlike a modern-era vehicle with its 12-volt battery, a Model A had only a 6-volt battery system with a positive ground. Still I was always able to coax the engine to start in even the most severe conditions.

Here are a few of the things I did to start the Model A:

Parked the vehicle in a sheltered area out of the wind.

In early winter, adjusted the voltage regulator so that the generator (Model A trucks didn't have a modern alternator) would create a higher-voltage current. The ampere gauge was the only standard gauge on the Model A's petite dash.

Changed the engine oil seasonally. In early winter, #20 oil (fall and spring oil) was drained and #10 oil was put in the crankcase. When temperatures reached minus 20 degrees, the

#10 oil was thinned with one cup of kerosene. When minus 30 degrees was reached, a second cup of kerosene was used to dilute the oil to further reduce resistance while attempting to crank the engine over in the starting procedure.

When in doubt that the engine would start because of extreme cold, especially on the Gunflint, I draped a huge canvas over the entire front end of the truck. The canvas covered the radiator, engine hood, both front fenders, and front bumper.

It was vitally important that the canvas hang down on the ground. Next, I positioned a one-gallon metal can filled with burning charcoal under the engine and blocked it in place up against the bottom of the engine's oil pan. The concentrated intense charcoal heat rose and heated the massive iron engine and its oil.

The canvas trapped the heat, which in turn helped heat the battery. Within one hour, the warm microclimate freed the frozen grasp nature had claimed on the engine, allowing it to turn over easily and sputter to life. (Note: The truck's battery had been removed from under the cab's floorboards and mounted on the firewall under the hood.)

My last starting aid was to set the gasoline flow from the carburetor to the engine in an enriched position. This could be done with the choke knob from the inside of the cab while I adjusted the spark lever and depressed the floor starter switch.

When the Model A sputtered to life, my proud smile and enthusiasm was as huge as the bright sun which usually accompanied bitter temperatures. Travel was now possible, whether my aim was to go explore, fish on another lake, or return to Duluth.

8
Rural Traditions

A sortie is a mission or attack by plane. Just as I had destinations in the summer via the Model A, so I had many sorties to lakes in the winter. These trips frequently resulted in having to use tire chains and snow shovel to extricate the truck from wind-blown snowdrifts.

One mid-morning in December, after starting the Model A, I ventured from West Bearskin toward Clearwater Lake. Halfway there, a distance of about a mile, I met three men cutting birch firewood for Charlie and Petra Boostrom. I couldn't help but to stop and ask if I could help.

I'm sure the men asked themselves what I could do with such a tiny truck. Before long, I parked the Model A.

Each man had a job. Glen Boostrom was operating a dozer. He would go into the woods, cut a mature birch, and drag it close to the road. Bobby Leonard skillfully cut the logs into firewood length with a chainsaw without pinching the saw's bar or dulling the chain by striking the ground. Neil Hall would lift the massive chunks into the bed of his pickup truck

View from Model A on Clearwater Lake en route to Mountain Lake.

One of the many log cabins in the Gunflint Trail area.

and quickly haul them half a mile to the Boostrom home.

I stayed clear of all the power equipment and assisted Neil. By the end of the day, a winter's fuel supply sat alongside the Boostrom home. The next day I returned to assist the men in splitting the huge pile.

That opportunity to help was a blessing. I thoroughly enjoyed the workout of lifting firewood, getting my choppers, pants, and coat somewhat soaked from melting snow. The family was extremely grateful. Many times I was invited to huge festive dinners fixed on a woodstove. And many times, when I sought advice or help, I was welcomed like family.

Recognizing my rambunctiousness, Glen warned me where not to travel or explore on the lakes with the Model A.

"Islands are bad," were his first words.

Many lakes on the Gunflint were considered deep-water bodies when compared to the lakes of central Minnesota. Thus, they froze later.

"Never go on a lake with a vehicle until there is 12 inches of ice" was another piece of good advice, as springs and water currents create thinner ice. And, he said sternly, "Don't even think you can cross ice at the mouths or inlets of even small creeks. Billy Needham puts up his summer ice supply around Christmas. After a dusting of snow and a gust of wind, you can't tell where the icebox ice was taken from the lake."

"Another bad place is around beaver houses," he shared from trapping experience. As a result of his advice, I didn't venture out on to Gunflint lakes unless another vehicle had already done so.

Residents of Cook County did get excited about ice fishing. Since snowmobiles had yet to be invented, fishermen ventured out on the ice with vehicles if there was little snow and no slush. More than once, I followed the vehicle tracks of Neil Hall down Clearwater Lake to the Mountain Lake portage, parked on the ice, and snowshoed over the portage to ice fish.

Years ago there used to be winter portages. These portages weren't for vehicles, but rather for winter ice-fishing enthusiasts to safely skirt river currents and thin ice on snowshoes to get to their favorite lakes.

I learned to appreciate snowshoes. Often, by the end of a winter season, I would have to relace the wooden snowshoe frames with new rawhide lacing.

I was once invited to go ice fishing on Little Saganaga Lake. It was a long snowshoe trip. We avoided thin ice, above which wisps of water vapor danced in the subzero temperatures, by crossing winter portages.

For two evenings we stayed in a one-room cabin heated by a barrel stove. It was on that winter adventure with the Boostroms that I learned the whereabouts of numerous private cabins, trapping shacks, and fishing shanties in the greater Gunflint area. Swan, Gaskin, Winchell, Long Island, Fraser, Seagull, Saganagons, Ross, Greenwood, Northern Light, Granite, North, Rose, Mountain, Baker and Moose are just a few of the lakes I visited with cabins.

Some of these cabins were absolutely unique. Log cabins with birch-bark roofs. A cabin with three log walls, one plank wall, and a rough-sawn lumber roof. Others with beautiful stone fireplaces. These structures represented dreams, endless ambition, and pioneer spirit. Today, hardly any evidence exists of what I observed.

9
Moose Meat

It was a midwinter night on the Gunflint Trail. The road surface was glazed ice from a February rain followed by temperatures dropping below freezing. Fortunately, I was traveling with extreme caution that slippery night when I came upon an accident scene.

This was no ordinary in-the-ditch accident. This accident was the result of a vehicle colliding with a moose, or vice versa.

There was only one undamaged vehicle present, parked at the side of the road. A small emergency beacon pierced the still, foggy environment. Cautiously I steered the Model A to a halt along the slippery shoulder.

Down in the ditch I noticed the beam of a flashlight. Unable to identify anyone behind the flashlight beam, I chose to investigate. There, all by himself in the ditch, I met the game warden, Bill Zickrick.

He had propped his flashlight in the snow bank. The beam light, shrouded by wisps of drifting fog, focused on a magnificent moose.

Bill explained the accident scenario while he straightened his weary back. He had received a call from the sheriff's office just prior to the supper hour. The driver and passenger of the vehicle had to be taken to Duluth for life-threatening injuries. The totally destroyed vehicle had been towed to town. He learned that the moose had struggled to get off the highway and could not be seen in the dark by the tow truck operator.

That was about five hours ago. After Bill's initial investigation, upon which he found the moose dead, it was his responsibility as the state's DNR officer to dispose of the moose as he deemed possible per regulations. What he did before he left town was to notify a party, both for assistance and to lay claim to the moose per his discretion. Now, several hours later, with the moose 90 percent skinned and quartered, I had appeared in the Model A truck.

Fascinated by the circumstances, I volunteered my assistance. There was no refusing by the officer. While we struggled to get the gigantic quarters up to the road, he explained that I was the only vehicle to come along since he got to the accident scene. This didn't surprise me! After each piece we got to the roadside, we gasped and leaned on his vehicle. After each trip we huffed and made small talk. To me, this was an unbelievable situation. However, as Bill explained, with the Minnesota moose herd growing rapidly, such unfortunate encounters were occurring monthly.

Now more than an hour had passed since I arrived at the scene. According to Bill, what he wanted to salvage from the moose was at the roadside and no help had come. He had really gone beyond his duties. He was soaked from both snow and exhaustion. He was dedicated beyond belief while he ate his sandwich (actually his supper) and pondered his next move.

Time passed slowly while we discussed the area in his truck. Finally, probably in frustration, he asked, "How would you like some moose meat?"

"Sure," leapt out of my mouth. Eagerly I followed him to

the pile of meat. Unbelievable!

First, I rearranged the contents of the Model A's little box. Then we hoisted a front shoulder into the box.

"Do you want more?"

Quickly thinking the family would really appreciate the meat, my response was affirmative. Bill generously gave me another colossal hunk. I was thrilled to help him load the remaining moose into his pickup box.

Before we parted in opposite directions, he to Grand Marais and I up the Gunflint Trail to my cabin, I sensed utter frustration that no assistance came from town. However, he was very professional and appreciative of my help.

Whatever amount of moose meat I had in the box of the tiny pickup provided increased traction on the Trail to my cabin. I even had to downshift on the uphill grades. It wasn't until in daylight the next day did I realize the magnitude of the moose.

Literally two huge quarters took up the entire box. What a sight! Two moose hooves hanging over the end of the tailgate.

10
Breakdowns

People have asked me if I ever had a breakdown in the Model A that left me stranded. The answer is yes. Fortunately, though, they occurred in some season other than winter. Each time, I was blessed to be aided by someone I helped in prior years.

Breakdown #1 occurred on Clearwater Road in late June. As Bill Johanson and I passed Aspen Annie's little resort on the Clearwater Road, the Model A coughed and wheezed, nearly jerking to a stop. I downshifted to first gear and limped up the hill behind Barney Varap's Aspen Lake cabin.

At the top of the hill, the engine was backfiring terribly and we couldn't continue. I tried to restart the engine, but it was a hit-and-misfire situation. I opened the hood and saw nothing out of place. I don't believe Bill ever had faith in the old relic and his face spoke volumes.

I, too, began to question my options. Here we were, three miles from the cabin and broken down. When Bill and I were about to strike out on foot down the road to West Bearskin, Neil Hall stopped to offer help.

Of course, he recognized the truck and from his window hollered, "Have you got problems, Bob?"

What luck! Everybody in Cook County knew of Neil's mechanical prowess. It wasn't long before he diagnosed a blown head gasket. Even better yet, he believed that in Charlie Boostrom's tool house, a Model A head gasket hung on the wall.

He volunteered to go and get it, and within a half hour had returned with proper wrenches. It was a used gasket. Before an hour passed, the head gasket was replaced and we drove off to the cabin.

How grateful I was. "That's OK," Neil kept saying as I thanked him over and over. "You've helped us haul and split firewood many times."

There are people who are happy helping fix other people's mechanical problems; Neil Hall was one such person. Ever since Breakdown #1, I have carried a spare head gasket in the cab behind the seat. Oh, thank heavens Model A parts were as common as rocks on the North Shore of Lake Superior.

Breakdown #2 also involved a bit of good fortune. It just so happened that I left Duluth bound for the Gunflint on Friday morning rather than Thursday night. About midday, after fueling up at the Holiday Service station, I was headed up the long hill out of Grand Marais when the engine just quit.

On the wide shoulder I tried to restart the engine, but all it would do was spin over. Again hood up, both sides, no obvious broken parts or wires disconnected.

This time, Grand Marais was closer than the cabin. I let the Model A roll downhill to gain momentum. Next, I backed across the highway, pointed the box uphill, and finally let gravity carry the truck downhill. Still the truck wouldn't start by popping the clutch with the transmission in third gear.

Plan B was to coast downhill and get close to the Holiday station, where I would ask Mike Quaife if I could use his phone to call Duluth. Graciously, Mike allowed me to make a long-distance call to my folks.

Divine intervention must have planned this breakdown. Late this afternoon, my parents had planned to come north to the cabin for the weekend. Like Neil Hall, my dad had ample Model A mechanical expertise. He would come with possible repair parts and tools.

That afternoon, the Model A sat on Highway 61 near the Dairy Queen. Tourists walked by, motorists honked, and I enjoyed three DQ cones. Help was on the way.

Parts, tools and Dad arrived by six o'clock. Soon he had determined that the problem was not electrical. Could the teeth be stripped on the timing gear?

Sure enough, when the timing plate on the engine was removed, the teeth on the gear were sheared off. Dad instructed me to jack up one rear wheel, preferable the curbside wheel. Because the winch welded to the front bumper blocked the crankshaft crank hole, the engine had to be turned slowly by rotating a rear-drive wheel with the transmission in high or third gear. When the crankshaft timing mark aligned with the timing shaft mark, and the #1 piston was up on the compression stroke, Dad slid the new gear into place.

With all the parts in place and the rear wheel on the ground, I was given the command to start the truck. Yes! On the first revolution the lethargic engine became conscious and animated.

Later that weekend I learned that the stripped gear was made of fiberglas. Original timing gears were cast of a durable aluminum alloy. The metal was durable, but noisy. Aftermarket products produced quieter fiberglass timing gears that were substantially less durable. That evening, Dad installed a metal gear. To tell the truth, noise-wise, I couldn't perceive a difference. But from then on I carried an extra timing gear under the seat.

Breakdown #3 started with a crunch.

Late in the month of October, while grouse hunting, I drove down a short, frosty logging road that led to a recent clear cut. At the clear cut, rather than stop, reverse, turn around and exit, I drove in a short circle at the log landing before exiting.

Crunch! The left rear wheel fell in a large hole.

Stuff flew all over the inside of the cab: ice scrapers, pliers, tools, extra wiper blade, shotgun shells, water bottle, pencil and map. The cushion seat became dislodged. Dust flew. Mayhem briefly reigned.

The jolt of such a drop and the resulting mess in the cab thrust my right foot down hard on the floor accelerator pedal. Luckily, the Model A bounced forward out of the deep hole. I stopped on the logging road to reorganize the cab and inspect for damage. Seeing no apparent damage, I proceeded to hunt the rest of the day.

Well, late that afternoon, somewhere on the original Greenwood Road once again, the left rear wheel of the truck fell clattering and scraping to the gravel roadbed. Before the Model A had screeched to a halt, much to my astonishment, the left rear wheel—complete with mechanical brake drum and broken axle shaft—rolled and wobbled past the cab and into the ditch.

Fear, shock, and instant thoughts of being stranded near dusk ramped up the adrenaline in my system. There was no moving the truck off the roadbed. There was no real prospect of another vehicle coming along, either.

Walking is good; it gives you time to ponder. I knew little about who waited back at Greenwood Lake, if anybody, at that time of year. Thus, I stashed what gear I thought was relevant in a #2 Duluth pack. With my .410 shotgun in hand, I struck out walking and jogging the six miles to the Gunflint Trail.

Focused on reaching the Trail before nightfall, I passed opportunities to shoot grouse on the way. My mind was doing advanced problem-solving the whole way. Once I reached the wide Brule River, which I waded across, I knew the Gunflint was only a couple of blocks away. From there, I perceived my best option was to walk to West Bearskin.

Vehicle traffic was almost nonexistent on the Gunflint Trail while I walked. One station wagon went past, going up the Trail. Another sedan was headed for Grand Marais. After hiking probably three miles on the Trail, I heard a vehicle.

Its headlights were on. The last rays of dusk filtered through the conifers. I was famished. Just before the truck swept past me, I raised my free hand to wave.

The brake lights lit up first, then the white reverse lights. I had hardly noticed the damp autumn chill in the air when I thought I recognized the burnt-orange Chevy truck. Could that be Bobby Leonard's truck?

"What in the hell are you doing here? Get in!" boomed his stout voice. It had been at least three years since I last saw him cutting birch on the Clearwater Road. Certainly he was headed for Clearwater. What a fortuitous fate suddenly befell upon me after breakdown #3.

From Boostrom's via phone I was able to reach a college friend, Frank Helquist. Frank enjoyed fishing and had stayed with me on occasions when he and buddies fished the Gunflint. (Frank's mother, as a young girl in the 1920s, had ridden as a passenger on the train from Duluth all the way to Rose Lake.) I had to give directions to him to pick up a car trailer from my uncle Kenny's in Duluth Heights.

The next morning, I met Frank at the West Bearskin landing. Together he and I traversed the back roads in his Plymouth Fury, car trailer in tow, until we approached the paralyzed Model A. With chain come-a-longs we managed to drag the truck onto the trailer. That evening, when my parents returned home from southern Minnesota, I explained my ill-fated adventure.

Those were the only major breakdowns I experienced in some 58,703 miles of pocket-book adventures in northern Minnesota. Minor issues, including flat tires, clogged carburetor sediment bowl, and a fouled spark plug, maybe have delayed forward momentum on trips, but were fairly easily diagnosed and remedied.

Thank you, Henry Ford, for creating the phenomenal, versatile American icon simply called the Model A.

11
Parts and Title

The homespun 1930 Model A truck was one of many Model A trucks my father acquired and restored. In fact, for many years he maintained—in running and national-award-winning condition—every model of the 1930 Model A that Ford Motor Company manufactured.

To support his Model A fleet, he was constantly purchasing parts from farmers, junkyards, defunct dealerships and abandoned homesteads.

Soon his automobile collection outgrew his 40-foot by 100-foot garage. Three more buildings were erected. However, after five decades of collecting, he had to downsize and dispose of his vehicles. At that time, he offered me any vehicle in his collection.

My decision was quick and obvious: the Model A pickup. I passed on the valuable and rare models in favor of my old companion. It was rough and low in value as far as a collector piece, but kindled a lifetime of memories. When I retired and moved full-time to the Gunflint Trail, the pickup and a classic maroon four-door Model A sedan came with me.

The titles had to be transferred to my name. This was a problem. See, the serial number on the title certificate didn't match the serial number stamped on the engine block of the truck.

Of course it didn't. Dad would often rebuild or replace a well-worn engine for one in better condition. As a teenager,

I sometimes helped him switch out engines on a Saturday morning. We'd go for a ride in the vehicle after lunch.

After many telephone conversations with the Minnesota Motor Vehicle Division, I was finally granted a clear title to the Model A.

12

Vanishing Era

Traces of the past 60 years still exist at junctures along and about the Gunflint Trail. While hiking and hunting, I ask myself, "What has happened to the forest?"

Acres of dead birch snags. Huge blown-down trunks of many tree species lie crisscrossed on the forest floor. The tiny spruce budworm has taken a toll on the forest. Blackened silhouettes of trees and brush stand from fires, both natural and prescribed. White cedar tree fronds are thin and often lack the deep, forest-green color of healthy species of the past. Majestic, century-old white pines have dead tops.

These days as I saunter along, shotgun under my arm, on trails of golden popple leaves, I notice traces of the past. Once-navigable logging roads are now grown closed with species of brush: alder, willow, mountain maple, and hazel brush. On some routes, earthen berms are disguised with raspberry bushes. On other trails, huge rocks placed to restrict vehicle traffic are hidden by conifers. Railroad grades, too, have been reclaimed by nature. Only now, on crinkled parchment maps, are you able to witness the pathways of the past. These traces and old maps rekindle my memories.

Without a doubt, the Model A was a simple vehicle compared to modern ones. Here are a few other symbols of simplicity of a past era: single-shot shotguns, splitting maul, wood stove, water bucket, snow shovel, snow scoop, kerosene lanterns, and coffee percolator. When is the last time you heard a

Many all season trips started and ended here.

fisherman say he was going fishing with his cane pole?

To some people, the simple way of life may imply hard and maybe laborious work. But when things broke, they weren't hard or complicated to fix. I have learned to appreciate the simple things from Gunflint living. This philosophy was initiated by the 1930 Model A truck.

The last ride was as thrilling as the first. I give thanks to my wife, my family, and the inspiring, dauntless black Model A.

I hope that the focus of this rambling has been on the truck so it can live on in memory and imagination. I hope the Model A will forever be on the Gunflint Trail.

Oops, I forgot to tell you about getting the Model A stranded in water up to the dipstick and being pulled out by an

Oldsmobile. Oh well. Maybe it's for the better, since that era has passed.

Regardless of how much things have changed, I'd like to close with a quote from Lee Nelson Zopff, past owner of Clearwater Lodge and Canoe Outfitters. Early one summer, before the heavy influx of guests, fishermen and canoeists, a traveling salesman for the Fisher Map Company approached Lee.

At the lodge he was expounding on the virtues of the latest copyrighted maps he had to offer. After listening to him for quite some time, Lee rebuffed his offers and assured him she had plenty of maps from the last season, adding, "Besides, the lakes haven't changed. Nor have the portages."

Other Books from North Shore Press

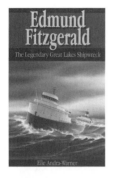

Edmund Fitzgerald
The Legendary Great Lakes Shipwreck
By Elle Andra-Warner
Softcover, $9.95

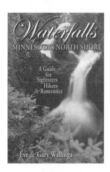

Waterfalls of Minnesota's North Shore
A Guide for Sightseers, Hikers, and Romantics
By Eve and Gary Wallinga
Softcover, $14.95

Superior Seasons
Life on a Northern Coast
By Shawn Perich
Softcover, $14.95